contents:

Introduction

This book is the sequel to my earlier publication, 'Raising Standards in Writing', ('Kirklees School Effectiveness Service, Huddersfield, Yorkshire'). That publication guides the reader through the process of a long term strategy to raise standards in writing, and introduces the strategies that can have a quick impact. This publication takes the quick impact strategies and further develops them, providing exemplar lesson plans, resources and teaching tips.

The contents of this book centre around the teaching of six lessons during the Spring Term in the lead up to the national tests for eleven year olds. A case study, (Horton Park Primary School) was given as illustration in the first publication. A further case study is provided in this publication, from the writer's work in a school in Bradford, Yorkshire. (See 'Usher Street Primary School')

This book does not aim to provide the Long Term Strategy described in 'Raising Standards in Writing'. However, 'The Criterion Scale' that is the assessment tool for targeted termly assessment is included in this publication because it gives teachers a clear, progressive picture of how the levels develop. If the Criterion Scale is used regularly to assess pupils' writing, the progression becomes embedded in the teacher's mind, and informs her / his teaching and responses to pupils' oral answers and writing.

The quick impact strategies have been proved to work repeatedly in schools across the country, as a result of colleagues attending courses or school-based training. Sometimes the impact is amazing, for example a case study in this book shows a seven year old pupil rising from a level 2C to 4C in one academic year through proactive teaching to the Four Generic Targets. (See 'High Crags Primary School Case Study').

There are still many teachers who feel that proactive teaching of strategies is an artificial route to raising standards, and who fear that it will suppress creativity. There is no evidence of the latter. The exemplification materials in this book are typical of the progress shown by most pupils, and evidence that as the skills of writing improve, so creativity improves. (See 'Usher Street' and 'High Crags' case studies.)

Standards are usually higher in the national tests for science than in mathematics and English. In many schools they are higher in mathematics than they are in English. In the majority of schools it is the scores in writing that suppress the English mark, often being ten percent or more below scores for reading. Skills in science and mathematics are taught proactively or 'scientifically' in a logical progression that raises standards. It is the premise of the writer of this book that skills in writing should be taught the same way. Just as the emerging mathematician or scientist has a limited grasp and ability to apply their embryonic skills, so does the emerging writer. As their repertoire expands, however, they mature into confident writers with a wide range of strategies at their disposal. Teachers should not withhold the proactive teaching many pupils require through fear that it is an 'artificial' process.

Ros Wilson
November 2002

> # Breaking through the glass ceiling
> of teacher expectation

Teachers who have adopted the scientific teaching of the skills of writing described in this book, have discovered that pupils can succeed as writers far beyond levels usually expected for their age. As noted in the introduction, skilful teaching that celebrates the achievement of each step in a progressive scale of skills and then systematically teaches the next skills in the scale has led to incredible results such as those seen in the High Crags Case Study.

Involving pupils in their own learning by sharing the secret garden of assessment with them, and explaining exactly what we are doing in terms of assessment, targeted assessment, setting of targets and measuring of progress, empowers and excites them. This is because we are now able to promise pupils that we will systematically teach the skills they need to rise up the 'league table' of success, and that if they will learn and use the bite size skills we are going to teach they will all become effective and successful writers.

The skilful teacher then makes the learning explicit through saying, 'If you do this, you will score goals in writing.' When you have scored x number of goals, (depending where within the scale the pupil is currently achieving) you will move up the league table. I will teach you each skill clearly, showing you how it is used and helping you to practise using it until you are confident, just like we teach you the skills of football.' This makes sense to pupils, and is particularly helpful in motivating many already disaffected by writing. It then becomes entirely natural for the teacher to continue the teaching through the progression, regardless of how highly the pupil is already scoring. That is the reason why a seven year old boy is empowered to attain level four in an aspect of English that boys do not traditionally enjoy.

Like many teachers, the writer spent her classroom career believing that if the pupils' skills of reading improved, their writing would improve also. It has become evident that around sixty percent of the population will never read widely enough, regularly enough, at a high enough challenge level or with enough pleasure to subconsciously absorb higher order structures and consciously apply them in writing. This is what most teachers and other professional people did as they were maturing through education, but they are representative of only forty percent of the population of the country.

Because that is how we learned these skills and strategies, we believe it is how all pupils will learn them. The evidence is that over half the pupils in our classes will not acquire the higher order skills unless we teach them explicitly and in the appropriate hierarchy.

Regular use of the Criterion Scale to assess writing and set personal targets for individual pupils, plus proactive teaching of the four generic targets, embeds the progression in the teacher's mind, so that she or he can respond precisely to each step of pupils' achievement through feedback, including through marking, in the periods between the termly targeted assessments recommended for the long term strategy.

Showing pupils the Criterion Scale, and telling them that you will give them their own copy when their writing reaches Level 5, is empowering for pupils. It should also be shared with parents, who will enjoy seeing the progress in their child's writing as evidenced through the pieces of writing in the pupil's plastic pocket in the school's portfolio of evidence. (See 'The Criterion Scale').

Proactive teaching to the four generic targets

Vocabulary, connectives, openers and punctuation are the VCOP, (see 'The Four Generic Targets') which should be taught systematically in lively, fun ways. The six lesson plans provided in this book provide a model for this teaching. They are not intended to be followed rigidly, and must be adapted for the age and ability of the pupils to be taught. These generic targets 'grow' or become more sophisticated as the child matures, and indeed - for many of us – into adulthood.

Most of us were not proactively taught how to use these features. Those of us who write at Level 5 skill level, (by which stage all the skills of writing are embedded and from then on increase in range, sophistication and challenge of context) have developed these features through our reading. This is true for most teachers, and explains why we believe that if we teach children to read better they will write better.

THE IMPORTANCE OF EMBEDDING

Level 3 is the level of daily writing for most adults. When we write to friends, plan lessons, leave notes at home or leave instructions for people at work we rarely write above Level 3 in terms of skills. This needs to be considered against the fact that sophistication in vocabulary is the only age related criteria in the Criterion Scale and in the Four Generic Targets. It is our vocabulary and confidence in applying skills that mainly define our writing as more mature. We usually only use our higher order skills when we want to impress, for example in formal letters, application forms and publications. However, because they are embedded from Level 5, they are always there and can be drawn upon at will, however infrequently they are used.

IF THEY DON'T USE IT THEY LOSE IT!

For pupils or adults still working towards Level 5, the features that raise levels are not embedded. If pupils do not use them regularly they will lose them. This is evidenced by the lowering of levels in writing BEFORE pupils leave their primary schools and enter secondary education. When the national tests are finished many teachers change the curriculum, and expectation of standards in writing is often lowered. Just as we forget how to calculate some of the more obscure features of mathematics because we do not use them in our lives, (for example, algebraic formula) many pupils forget the strategies to raise their level of writing.

The writer has evidence from two hundred pieces of unsupported writing from fourteen different primary schools, written in July 2002. This writing was given high significance by being a letter to the secondary school that the pupils were transferring to, yet almost sixty percent of pupils had 'dipped' in level since taking their national writing test in May.

INVOLVE PUPILS IN THE ASSESSMENT

A key factor in raising levels for pupils is their involvement in the process of assessment. All pupils from Year 1 up should know that there is an assessment tool that their teachers use to tell them what levels they are working at. They should know about levels, in the broad sense of the word, and should be able to evaluate text, recognising that one piece is at a higher level than another. These are important aspects of the six exemplar lesson plans in this publication.

Pupils who understand the impact their use of the VCOP has on the level of their writing often make rapid progress in writing. (See 'The Positive Writing Ethos')

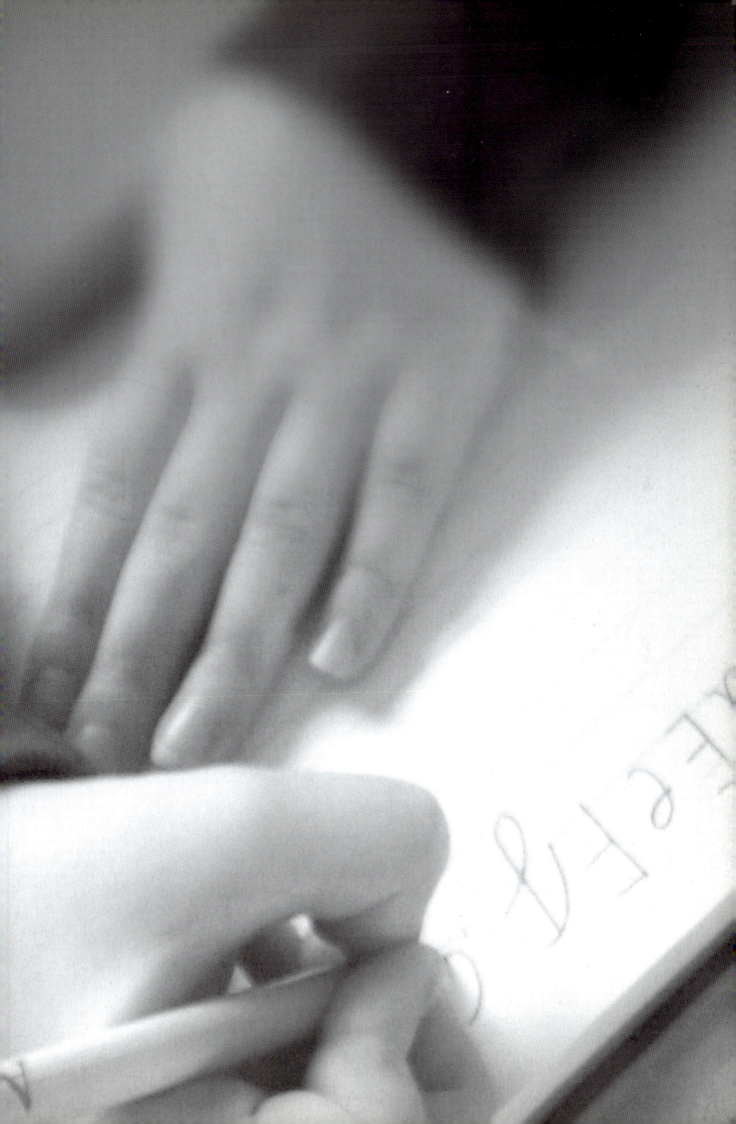

Rising through the levels

It is more useful to think of Level 2C as an extension of Level 1, as writing at 2C is more like Level 1 writing than it is like Level 2B or above. Writing at 2C is often little more than a paragraph of five or six sentences. It is frequently in a crude handwriting style with inaccurate sentence structure and/or use of full stops. Vocabulary is often basic and the content is sometimes still a series of simple statements. Writing at Level 2B is usually around one side in length, with basic sentence punctuation accurate at least 80% of the time. The writer uses extended sentences and may be beginning to consciously change the structure of sentences. He or she has a wider range of sight words that can be spelt accurately, and will be developing strategies for spelling unfamiliar words.

The journey from entry to Level 1 to secure 2C is a rapid one for many pupils with proactive teaching. **(See 'Progression in Teaching and Learning' AND 'The Writing Journey')**

NB: Pupils must make continuous progress in spelling and handwriting throughout the primary phase until they all reach a level of acceptable competency.

Spelling: they have a wide sight vocabulary and a range of strategies for building unknown words and can use a dictionary with confidence

Handwriting: they have a confident cursive style that is easily legible.

PROGRESSION IN TEACHING AND LEARNING

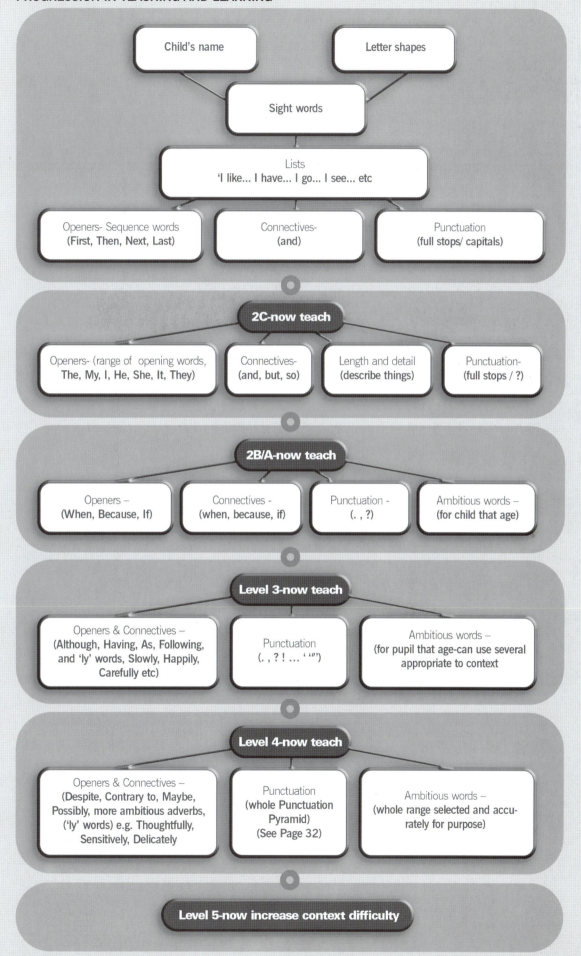

Child's name

Letter shapes

Sight words

Lists
'I like... I have... I go... I see... etc

Openers- Sequence words
(First, Then, Next, Last)

Connectives-
(and)

Punctuation
(full stops/ capitals)

2C-now teach

Openers- (range of opening words,
The, My, I, He, She, It, They)

Connectives-
(and, but, so)

Length and detail
(describe things)

Punctuation-
(full stops / ?)

2B/A-now teach

Openers –
(When, Because, If)

Connectives -
(when, because, if)

Punctuation -
(. , ?)

Ambitious words –
(for child that age)

Level 3-now teach

Openers & Connectives –
(Although, Having, As, Following,
and 'ly' words, Slowly, Happily,
Carefully etc)

Punctuation
(. , ? ! ... ' ")

Ambitious words –
(for pupil that age-can use several
appropriate to context

Level 4-now teach

Openers & Connectives –
(Despite, Contrary to, Maybe,
Possibly, more ambitious adverbs,
('ly' words) e.g. Thoughtfully,
Sensitively, Delicately

Punctuation
(whole Punctuation
Pyramid)
(See Page 32)

Ambitious words –
(whole range selected and accurately for purpose)

Level 5-now increase context difficulty

The writing journey

To raise the level of writing from Level 1 to 2C a pupil generally needs to do the following:
• Learn different words to start sentences, for example the sequence words,
  'First', 'Then' 'Next' and 'Last' or 'Finally'.
• Learn to use at least one connective, for example 'and' or 'but'.
• Begin to use full stops, although they may not be placed accurately
• Continue to learn sight words and spelling structures to expand their vocabulary

To raise the level of writing from a 2C to a 2B and above a pupil generally needs to do the following:
• increase the length through adding detail and description
• use more than one type of connective to extend sentences
• vary the way sentences open
• use sentence punctuation reasonably accurately

From that point onwards the pupil generally needs to:
• increase the range and sophistication of vocabulary
• increase the range and sophistication of sentence connectives
• increase the range and sophistication of sentence openers
• increase the range and accuracy of punctuation used

These are the four generic targets that are common to all levels of writing from 2B upwards, and from Level 5 they are the elements that increase the sophistication of writing. It is the person's repertoire and confidence in applying these four elements in increasingly challenging contexts that raises the level of writing from Level 5 upwards.

The following sections are reprints from the earlier publication, 'Raising Standards In Writing', (Kirklees School Effectiveness Service, Tel: 01484 225793). They are:

1. The Criterion Scale:
This is an accurate, formative assessment scale. If used to assess a pupil's piece of unsupported writing, it will tell the assessor what the pupil needs to do next to improve. This should be shared with the pupil, who should then be reminded of his/her targets each time s/he writes.

2. The Four Generic Targets:
These are the VCOP that should be taught systematically in lively, fun ways. The six lesson plans provided in this book are a model for this teaching. They are not intended to be followed rigidly, and must be adapted for the age and ability of the pupils to be taught.

This scale has been generated from the range of national materials listed in the source box for each level. It was written for the long-term strategy of raising standards in writing described in the first publication, ('Raising Standards in Writing', Kirklees School Effectiveness Service). Its use can be exemplified by studying the assessed exemplars of children's writing in this book. (See 'High Crags Case Study')

IT IS GENERIC AND CAN BE USED AGAINST ANY TEXT TYPE. WHEN USED EFFECTIVELY IT GIVES AN ACCURATE CORRESPONDENCE TO NATIONAL TEST CRITERIA.
For optional tests and past year's tests use the QCA criteria.

Structure:
• Each level has been broken down into specific criteria against which work can be assessed. The criteria from Level 1 to Level 5 have been sub-divided into three sections which give an indication of common performance at the sub-levels, C (low), B (secure) and A (high). Many children will, however, be demonstrating skills at all three sub-levels at one time, whilst still not having skills at sub-levels below their main level of attainment. It is for this reason that a 'best fit' judgement must be made, and the point score system in the 'Assessment' box gives an indicator of the sub-level demonstrated. It should be regarded as an indicator to within a point each side, as ephemeral factors such as voice, style and confidence will significantly affect the judgement. These factors are often as important or more important than any specific skill, but cannot be described in specific criteria. They can usually only be identified in applying assessment to a specific piece of writing.

• **On each page from Level 1 to Level 5 there is a 'Pre-requisite' box. Up to Level 3 these are criteria that must be included in the scale, if not already evidenced, as they are not present at that level. For each criteria added, an additional point must be added into the Assessment scale at the A sub-level. For Level 4 and 5 the pre-requisites become essential pre-entry criteria to protect standards and quality.**

This version of the criteria for assessing writing in English has been standardised in the assessment of over 20,000 pieces of children's writing spanning the Levels 'W', to 5 and has been successfully applied in the assessment and moderation of 600 samples by over 50 teachers across the Reception Year and Key Stages 1, 2 and 3.

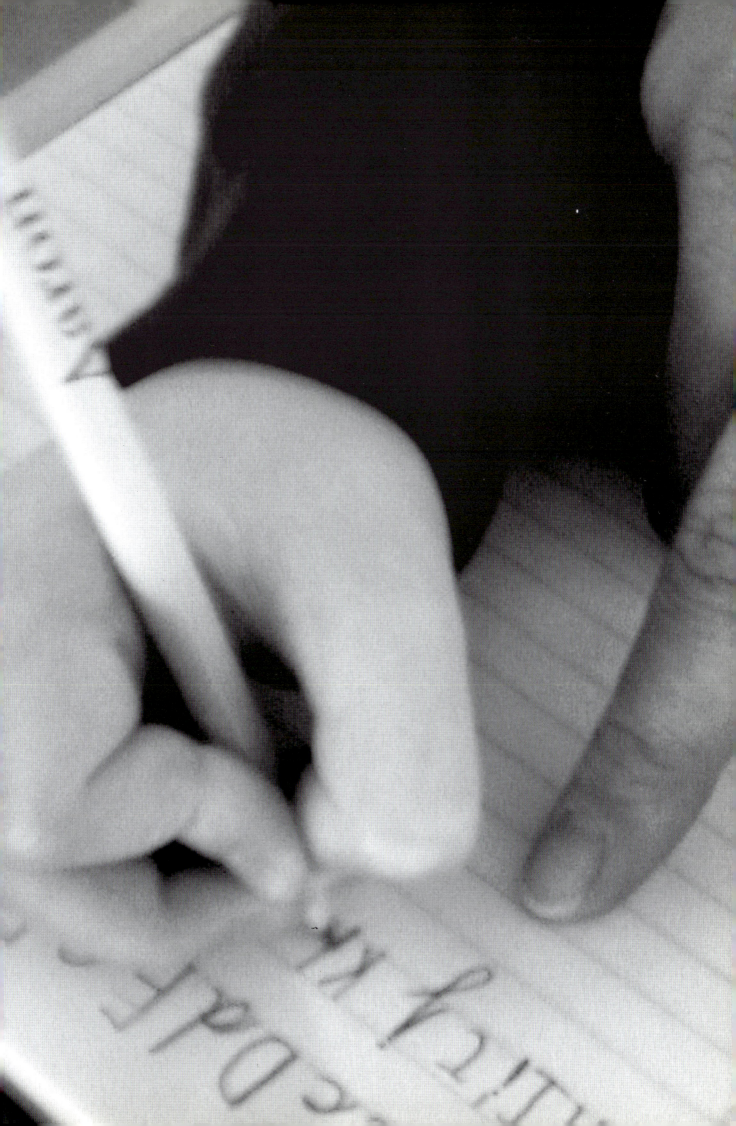

Sources:
Early Learning Journey
Performance Criteria (P Scales) for SEN
Curriculum Guidance For The Foundation Stage
NC Level Descriptions

Assessment:
$0 - 15 \quad = $ **W**
$18 - 26 = $ **W +**
W+ $\quad = $ **consider L1**
$20 - 26 = $ **assess for L1**

WORKING TOWARDS LEVEL 1 (W1) Criterion Scale
Listed in an approximate hierarchy.

The first ten criteria are in the pre-letter formation stage. If the child is making recognizable letter shapes they can be ticked off quickly.

- Will tolerate hand manipulation
- Will work with another to allow mark making using body parts or an implement
- Will attempt to mark make independently
- Can recognise mark making materials
- Can use and enjoys mark making materials
- Can show some control in mark making
- Can produce some recognisable letters
- Can write initial letter of own name
- Will attempt to 'write' things, including own name, using random letters
- Can differentiate between different letters and symbols
- Shows some awareness of sequencing of letters
- Will write own name but often with wrong letter formations or mixed lower / upper case
- Can copy over / under a model
- Can imitate adult's writing and understands the purpose of writing
- Is aware of different purposes of writing
- Can ascribe meaning to own mark making, ('reads' what has 'written')
- Knows print has meaning and that, in English, is read from left to right and top to bottom
- Can use a pencil and hold it effectively
- Can write own name with appropriate upper and lower case letters
- Can form most letters correctly
- Writes simple regular words
- Begins to make phonic attempts at words
- Writes captions, labels and attempts other simple forms of writing, (lists, stories etc)
- Can write single letters or groups of letters which represent meaning
- Can show some control over size, shape, orientation, in writing
- Can say what writing says and means

level 1

Sources:

Curriculum Guidance For The Foundation Stage
NC Optional Test Criteria and Guidance
QCA Exemplification of Standards Materials
NC Level Descriptions

Assessment:

MUST EVIDENCE CRITERIA '9' TO ATTAIN LEVEL 1

'9' + ANY 4 OTHERS (total 5)   = **1C**
'9' + 5 OR 6 OTHERS (total 6 / 7) = **1B**
'9' + 7 OR 8 OTHERS (total 8 /9) = **1A**
assess for level 2

Pre-requisite:

Can spell some common monosyllabic words correctly
(Level 1) Is decodable by an adult experienced in reading
early writing, without help from the child. (A few words
might not be decodable, but the 'gist' is clear).

LEVEL 1 Criterion Scale
- Can produce own ideas for writing
- Can write own name
- Can show some control over word order producing logical statements
- Can spell some common monosyllabic words correctly
- Can make recognisable attempts at spelling words not known, (most decodable without child's help)
- Can write simple text such as lists, stories, explanations
- Begin to show awareness of how full stops are used, in reading or in writing
- Can usually give letters a clear shape and orientation
- Can use simple words and phrases to communicate meaning (9) (ESSENTIAL - majority of work can be read / decoded by an adult without assistance from the child, must be more than one simple statement)

NB: FINAL NC CRITERIA, (9) IS ESSENTIAL TO ATTAIN 1C OR ABOVE

GUIDANCE:
AT MINIMUM THERE SHOULD USUALLY BE THREE OR MORE SIMPLE STATEMENTS OF THREE WORDS OR MORE EACH STATEMENT. A SIMPLE LIST OF STATEMENTS ALL STARTING WITH THE SAME KEY WORDS, (EG 'I CAN…' OR 'I LIKE……') CANNOT BE ASSESSED ABOVE 1C. THE ASSESSOR MUST BE CLEAR THAT THE CHILD HAS SELECTED THIS STRATEGY FOR PURPOSE, AND THAT IT IS NOT THE ONLY LIST THE CHILD IS ABLE TO PRODUCE, i.e. A ROTE LEARNED STRATEGY.

level1

Source:

NC Level Descriptions
Year 2 Task Criteria
Year 4 Optional Test Criteria
KS2 Mark Schemes

Assessment:

8 – 12 = **2C**
13 – 17 = **2B**
18 – 22 = **2A assess for Level 3**

Pre-requisites for Level 2: if not present must be included as additional criteria and the assessment thresholds increased by one

• Can use simple words and phrases to communicate meaning (9) (ESSENTIAL - majority of work can be read / decoded by an adult without assistance from the child, must be more than one simple statement)

LEVEL 2 Criterion Scale
Listed in an approximate hierarchy.

- Can write with meaning in a series of simple sentences, (may not be correct in punctuation and structure at 2C)
- Can produce short sections of developed ideas (2C may be more like spoken than written language)
- Can use appropriate vocabulary, (should be coherent and mainly sensible)
- Can use simple phonic strategies when trying to spell unknown words, (majority is decodable without child's help. If ALL spelling is correct – tick the criteria)
- Can control use of ascenders / descenders, upper / lower case letters in handwriting, although shape and size may not always be consistent
- Can use ANY connective, (may only ever be 'and') to join 2 simple sentences.

- Can communicate ideas and meaning confidently in a series of sentences
- Can usually sustain narrative and non-narrative forms (may not be sustained for 2C)
- Can provide enough detail to interest the reader, (e.g. is beginning to provide additional information or description)
- Can vary the structure of sentences to interest the reader, (e.g. has a number of ways for opening sentences that go beyond changing the first word - see the VCOP)
- Can use interesting and ambitious words sometimes, (should be words not usually used by a child of that age – see the VCOP)
- Can match organisation to purpose, (e.g. showing awareness of structure of a letter, openings and endings, importance of reader, organisational devices)
- Can usually use basic sentence punctuation (full stops followed by capital letters. If not 50% plus accurate, this bullet can only count towards the 8 needed for a 2C but not towards the 13 or more needed for B or A)
- Can use phonetically plausible strategies to spell or attempt to spell unknown polysyllabic words, (if all spelling is correct in a long enough piece to be secure evidence – tick the criteria).
- Can use connectives other than 'and' to join 2 or more simple sentences (e.g. but, so, then.)

- Can make writing lively and interesting
- Can link ideas and events, using strategies to create 'flow' (e.g. Last time, also, after, then, soon, at last, and another thing…)
- Can use adjectives and descriptive phrases for detail and emphasis
- Can usually structure basic sentences correctly, including capitals and full stops
- Can spell common monosyllabic words accurately
- Can use accurate and consistent handwriting, (in print at minimum, can use consistent use of upper / lower case, ascenders / descenders, size and form)
- Begins to show evidence of joining handwriting

Sectioned in approximate hierarchy of C, B, A. For assessment, however, the 'best fit' spans the three sections.

level2

Source:

NC Level Descriptions
Year 4 Optional Test Criteria
Exemplification Materials
KS2 Mark Schemes 2000

Assessment:
7 - 10   = **3C**
11 – 15 = **3B**
16 - 19 = **3A assess for Level 4**

Pre-requisite: if not yet present must be included as criteria for Level 3
• Can spell common monosyllabic words accurately, and use
  phonetically plausible strategies to attempt unknown polysyllabic
  words
• Can vary sentence structure
  (Level 2)
• Can sustain form to around 100 or more words

level3

LEVEL 3 Criterion Scale
Listed in an approximate hierarchy.

- Can produce work which is organised, imaginative and clear, (e.g. simple opening and ending)
- Can use a range of chosen forms appropriately and consistently, (e.g. letters – formal and informal, reporting, diary, dialogue)
- Can adapt chosen form to the audience, (e.g. provide information about characters or setting, make a series of points)
- Can use interesting and varied word choices, (MUST pick up on 'ambitious' from 2B)
- Can develop and extend ideas logically in sequenced sentences, (may still be overly detailed or brief)
- Can extend sentences using a wider range of connectives to clarify relationships between points and ideas, (e.g. when, because, if, after, while, also, as well)

- Can usually use correct grammatical structures in sentences, (nouns and verbs agree generally)
- Can use sentence punctuation accurately; full stops, capitals and question marks
- Can structure and organise work clearly, (e.g. beginning, middle, end; letter structure; dialogue structure)
- Can adapt form and style for purpose, (e.g. clear difference between formal and informal letters; abbreviated sentences in notes and diaries)
- Is experimenting with a wide range of punctuation, although use may not be accurate, (e.g. commas; inverted commas; exclamation marks; apostrophes)
- Can use cursive script accurately and neatly, although may be slow, (may not be accurate for Level 3C)

- Can use adjectives and adverbs for description
- Can spell common polysyllabic words accurately, (' sometimes' for Level 3C)
- Can develop characters and describe settings, feelings and emotions, etcetera
- Can link and relate events, including past, present and future, sensibly, (afterwards, before, also, after a while, eventually….)
- Can attempt to give opinion, interest or humour through detail
- Can use generalising words for style, (e.g. sometimes; never; always; often; in addition….)
- Is beginning to develop a sense of pace

Sectioned in approximate hierarchy of C, B, A. For assessment, however, the 'best fit' can span the three sections.

level3

level4

Source:
NC Level Descriptions
Year 4 Optional Tests
Exemplification Materials
KS2 Mark Schemes 2000

Assessment:
6 – 8   = **4C**
9 – 12 = **4B**
13 - 17 = **4A assess for Level 5**

Pre-requisite: if not yet present cannot be assessed for Level 4)
- Can use correct grammatical structures
- Can structure and punctuate sentences correctly (? . ,)
- Can use a range of connectives
- Can spell monosyllabic and common polysyllabic words correctly (Level 3)

LEVEL 4 Criterion Scale
Listed in an approximate hierarchy.

- Can write in a lively and coherent style
- Can use a range of styles confidently and independently
- Can use interesting language to sustain and develop ideas, (MUST pick up on 'ambitious' from 2B, may be using very adventurous language – sometimes inaccurately)
- Can organise ideas appropriately for both purpose and reader, (e.g. captions; headings; fonts; chapters; letter formats; paragraphs; logically sequenced events; contextual and background information etcetera)
- Can use full stops, question marks and commas accurately

- Can use more sophisticated connectives, (e.g. although, however, never the less)
- Can write in a clear, neat and legible cursive style
- Can produce thoughtful and considered writing, (uses simple explanation, opinion, justification and deduction)
- Can use or attempt grammatically complex structures, (e.g. expansion before and after the noun - 'The little, old man who lived on the hill..'; subordinating clauses – 'I felt better when..'; '…who taught me the guitar.')
- Can spell unfamiliar regular polysyllabic words accurately
- Can use nouns, pronouns and tenses accurately and consistently throughout

- Can use apostrophes and inverted commas, usually accurately
- Can select from a range of known adventurous vocabulary for a purpose, some words are particularly well chosen
- Can use connectives to give order or emphasis, (e.g. 'If…..then….'; 'We…..so as to…')
- Can select interesting strategies to move a story forward, (e.g. characterisation, dialogue with the audience, dialogue and negotiation within contexts etcetera)
- Can advise assertively, although not confrontationally, in factual writing, (e.g. 'An important thing to think about before deciding….'; 'We always need to think about….')
- Can develop ideas in creative and interesting ways

Sectioned in approximate hierarchy of C, B, A. For assessment, however, the 'best fit' can span the three sections.

level4

The Criterion scale
level5

Source:
NC Level Descriptions
Year 4 Optional Tests
Exemplification Materials
KS2 Mark Schemes 2000

Assessment:
9 – 12 = **5C**
13 – 17 = **5B**
18 – 22 = **5A assess for Level 6**

Pre-requisite: if not already present cannot be assessed for Level 5
- Can use nouns, pronouns and tenses accurately
- Can use a range of sentence punctuation accurately, (, . ? ' " ")
- Can use ambitious vocabulary (Level 4)
- Can vary the structure of sentences

level5

LEVEL 5 Criterion Scale
Listed in an approximate hierarchy.

- Can produce writing which is varied, interesting and thoughtful
- Can produce well structured and organised writing using a range of conventions in lay-out
- Can use appropriate informal and formal styles with confidence, (e.g. conversational, colloquial, dialectic, standard English)
- Can select from a wide range of known imaginative and ambitious vocabulary, and use precisely
- Can use paragraphs consistently and appropriately
- Can group subjects appropriately before or after a main verb, (e.g. The books, the pens and the pencils were all ready on the table
- Can use pronouns appropriately to avoid repetition when referring back or forward, (e.g. that, these, those, it)
- Can use different techniques to conclude work appropriately, (e.g. opinion, summary, justification, comment)
- Can use complex sentence structures appropriately
- Can use a range of punctuation, including commas, apostrophes and inverted commas accurately to clarify structure
- Can use punctuation appropriately to create effect, (e.g. exclamation marks, dashes, ellipses)
- Can write fluently in clear, joined script
- Can adapt handwriting for a range of tasks and purposes, including for effect
- Can use the passive voice for variety and to shift focus, (e.g. the cake was eaten by the child)
- Can show confident and established 'voice'
- Can use a range of narrative techniques with confidence, interweaving elements when appropriate, (e.g. action, dialogue, quotation)
- Can vary sentence length and word order confidently to sustain interest, (e.g. 'Having achieved your goals at such an early age, what motivates you to continue? Why fight on?)
- Can use a range of strategies and techniques confidently and appropriately to engage and involve the reader, (e.g. asides, comment, observation, anticipation, suspense, tension)
- Can use a range of devices to adapt writing to the needs of the reader, (e.g. parenthesis, introduction providing context, footnote, contents, bibliography)
- Can use literary features to create effect, (e.g. alliteration, onomatopoeia, figurative language, dialect)
- Can interweave implicit and explicit links between sections
- Can use punctuation to show division between clauses, to indicate, to vary pace, to create atmosphere or to sub-divide, (e.g. commas, colons, semi-colons, dashes, ellipses)

Sectioned in approximate hierarchy of C, B, A. For assessment, however, the 'best fit' can span the three sections

Strategies for Immediate Impact on Writing Standards

The four generic targets

There are 4 elements that are generic to all levels and sub-levels of development in writing skills. They are:

• the range of punctuation used
• the range of connectives used
• the range of sentence openers used
• the range of vocabulary and ambitious words used

There are many examples of all four of the generic elements that can be explicitly taught. For pupils, the above can be learned and used in context if well taught and embedded. The following analysis of progression in these generic targets is arbitrary and not definitive, and the examples given may have little resemblance to the evidence in an individual child's piece of work.

Different children will absorb and relate to these and other examples in differing sequences and to different degrees. They are intended as guidance only. In focusing on text in the Literacy Hour and story time, teachers should be raising awareness of ways that writers use these features to enrich their writing.

BACKGROUND TO THE FOUR GENERIC TARGETS (VCOP)

The criteria in the four generic targets are extracted from the Criterion Scale. The writer has used the Criterion Scale to assess over twenty thousand pieces of children's writing between October 1999 and October 2002. In setting three short-term targets for each pupil, it became evident that all pupils were receiving one or more of the four targets given here. This was true regardless of the age or level of writing skill of all pupils writing within Level 2 and above. This led to the realisation that there are four generic targets that 'grow' as the pupil's writing skill grows.

The following pages outline these four targets. The following analysis and exemplification is not definitive. It is guidance only. Different children will absorb and relate to these, and a wide range of other examples you will provide in differing sequences and to different degrees. Using all the opportunities at your disposal to focus on interesting examples of the VCOP will expand their repertoire so that the examples you find in their writing may not include many of the ones given here.

Some strategies for focusing on the VCOP are shown in the six exemplar lesson plans provided. Others are given at the end of this section of the book. (See 'Opportunities for Focusing on the Four Generic Targets')

NB: The targets are for your teaching. They are pitched increasingly high to increase the pace of progress, so that by secure level 3 and level 4 the pitch is one level higher. This is to allow for misuse through emergent strategies. Emergent misuse should be seen as a positive indicator of progress. (See 'The Positive Writing Ethos')

The four generic targets
Progress in Punctuation (See 'The Punctuation Pyramid')

Level 1 to 2C:

1. Recognition of full stops within texts.

2. Awareness that using full stops in writing is an important skill.

3. Use of random full stops; EITHER at the end of every line regardless of whether that is the end of a sentence or not, OR at any point within writing with no regard for sense.

Level 2B / 2A:

4. Uses full stops in the correct places more than 50% of the time

5. Uses a capital letter after a full stop consistently

6. Uses full stops in the correct places more than 80% of the time

Level 3:

7. Usually uses basic sentence punctuation, (full stops in the correct places – followed by capital letter) accurately, (around 90% of the time).

8. Uses a question mark accurately.

9. Experiments with use of commas, exclamation marks and sometimes apostrophes for contraction or possession

Level 4:

10. Uses sentence punctuation accurately, including question marks and exclamation marks.

11. Sometimes uses commas, apostrophes, (possessive and contraction) and inverted commas accurately.

12. Experiments with a wider range of punctuation and devices, which might include colons, semi-colons, dashes and ellipses.

Level 5:

13. Uses the full range of punctuation and devices, usually accurately and consistently.

> Strategies for Immediate Impact on Writing Standards

The four generic targets
Progression in Connection of Sentences

Level 1 and 2C:

1. Can join 2 simple sentences with 'and', (at the minimum. Accept ANY connective)

Level 2B / A:

2. Can use one or more connectives other than 'and', e.g. but, so, then…..

3. Can experiment with a wider range of connectives, e.g. because, if, when….

Level 3:

4. Can use a wider range of connectives within sentences, which might include several of the following; because, before, after, when, if, as well as…

5. Can use connectives to open sentences, e.g. Before, After, When, If, As well as…

6. Can experiment with a wider range of connectives, e.g. although, however, never the less….

Level 4:

7. Can use a range of connectives, usually accurately and consistently.

8. Can use connectives to make relationships between ideas and statements, e.g. also, in addition to, contrary to, despite……

9. Can experiment in the use of more ambitious connectives to open sentences e.g. Although…. Having…. Despite….

The four generic targets
Progression in Sentence Openers

Level 1 / 2C:

1. Opens simple statements and sentences with 'The…' 'My…' and 'I…'

Level 2B / A:

2. Can open sentences in a number of ways to show sequence, e.g. 'First…''Then…' Next…' 'Soon…' 'After that…' 'Last….'

3. Can open sentences with one or more connective e.g. 'Then'

4. Can open sentences with a range of connectives, e.g. 'Because…' ''If…' 'When…' 'After…'

5. Can experiment with sentence openers to link ideas and events, e.g. 'Last time…' 'Also…' 'After…' 'Soon…' 'Another thing…'

Level 3:

6. Can use sentence openers from Level 2 with accuracy.

7. Can use connectives to open sentences, e.g. Before, After, When, If, As well as…

8. Can use more sophisticated connectives to open sentences, e.g. 'Although…' After a while…'

9. Can use adjectives to create interest in openers, e.g. 'The golden sun shone…' 'Jane's favourite book….' 'Barking dogs…..'

10. Can experiment with use of noun phrases to open sentences, e.g. ' The little, old man who…'

Level 4:

11. Can experiment in the use of more ambitious connectives to open sentences e.g. Even if…. Having…. Despite….

12. Can use phrases in apposition to open sentences, e.g. 'Although I had thought that…, I discovered…' 'Having decided to…. I actually….' 'Despite James's plan to… in reality he…'

13. Can use contextual phrases of time, place or scenario to introduce ideas and events, e.g. 'Due to the lack of…. my first thought was to…' 'As the weather had become quite stormy, we decided to….' 'Before the audience left, the presenter asked…'

> ## The four generic targets
> ## Range of Interesting
> ## and Ambitious Vocabulary Used

This is more difficult to exemplify, as the range is exhaustive. The teacher's definition of 'ambitious' is crucial. This should mean:

A word not usually used by a child at this age or stage of development prior to proactive teaching.

Examples:

Age 5/6:

• Use of connectives e.g. 'because' and 'so'

• Use of sentence openers for time scale, e.g. 'First…' 'Next…'

• Use of words like ' exciting' 'interesting' 'afraid' 'lonely'

Age 6/7:

• Use of connectives / openers from Level 2B/A

• Use of adjectives like 'beautiful'…'awful'….'enormous'…'worst'….'fierce'

• Use of words like 'adventure' 'accident' 'magic'

Age 7/8:

• Use of connectives / openers from Level 3

• Use of adjectives like 'gigantic' 'weird' 'freezing'

• Use of adverbs like 'quietly' 'silently' 'bravely'….

• Use of abstract nouns like 'happiness' 'joy' 'sadness' 'fear'

• Use of nouns like 'transport' 'shelter' 'baggage' 'companion' 'vehicle'

The four generic targets
Range of Interesting
and Ambitious Vocabulary Used cont

Age 8/9:

- Use of connectives / openers from Level 3A and beyond

- Use of adjectives like 'thunderous' 'fearful' 'marvellous' 'attractive'

- Use of adverbs like 'generously' 'nervously' 'worriedly' 'patiently'

- Use of abstract nouns like 'feelings' 'courage' 'experience' 'patience' 'echo'

- Use of nouns like 'peak' 'wasteland' 'container' 'furnishings' 'robe'

Age 9/10:

- Use of a wide range of sophisticated connectives and openers

- Use of adjectives / adverbs like ' sensitive/ly' 'timid/ly' 'aggressive/ly' 'imaginative/ly'

- Use of adjectives such as 'unfortunate' 'murderous' 'echoing' 'doubtful'

- Use of abstract nouns like 'emotion' 'anxiety' 'longing' 'progress'

- Use of nouns like 'system' 'communication' 'ingredient' 'vibration'

- Use of verbs like 'prefer' 'nourish' 'demonstrate' 'enjoy' 'leap'

Age 10/11:

- Use of a wide range of sophisticated connectives and openers

- Use of adjectives / adverbs such as 'outstanding/ly' 'tender/ly' 'biological/ly

- Use of adjectives such as 'formidable' 'outspoken' 'stern' 'comical' 'pathetic'

- Use of verbs like, 'dwell' 'dine' 'progress' 'create' 'adore'

- Use of abstract nouns such as 'premonition ' 'yearning' 'speculation'

- Use of nouns such as 'silhouette' 'terrain' 'apparel' 'vision' 'apparition'

> # The four generic targets
> ## Opportunities for the four generic targets

1. As a 'Warm Up' before a literacy hour. Use of VCOP cards for a few minutes each day will accelerate progress. (See LSMs 8:2 and exemplar lesson plans.)

2. Last few minutes 'fillers' as in 1.

3. In guided reading. Take the opportunity to comment on interesting examples of VCOP.

4. In guided writing / unsupported writing. Prompt pupils, 'Remember your VCOP' and praise any use. (See exemplar lesson plans).

5. In text level work within the literacy hour. Take every opportunity to comment on interesting examples of VCOP.

6. In story time. Praise pupils who spot interesting use of VCOP.

7. In your modelling of writing for all purposes. Take every opportunity to comment on or exemplify interesting examples of VCOP.

8. In reading texts for all subjects. Take every opportunity to comment on interesting examples of VCOP.

9. When scaffolding work for pupils. Include and comment on features of VCOP.

10. When pupils are planning their writing. Encourage them to be pre-thinking about the features of VCOP they will use. (See, 'Planning Writing')

> The four generic targets
The Punctuation Pyramid

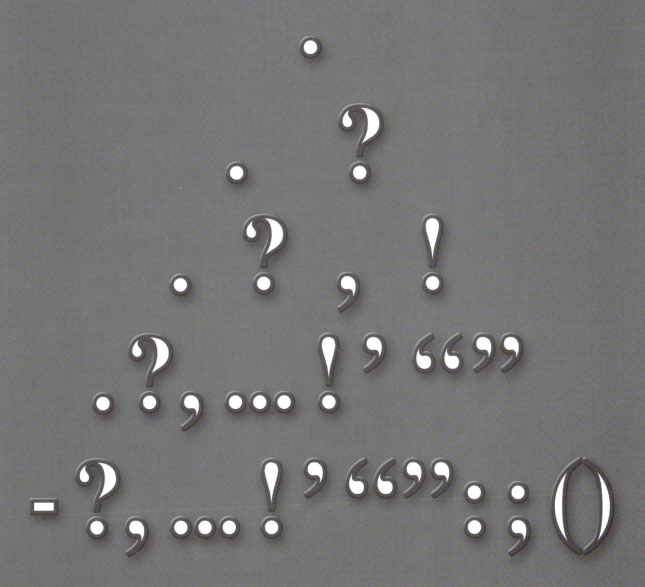

Use to illustrate progression in punctuation. Ask pupils to guess what the pyramid represents. Steer towards 'levels'. Name all punctuation. These may be added.

Refer to it every time pupils write in any subject. Play games by covering items with post-its and asking what is covered. Work towards pupils knowing level 5 by heart.

This exercise should be lively and fun. Pupils should be constantly praised and rewarded with 'training goals' or washed grapes.

> # Increasing length through detail and description

The Story Structure Cards, (LSMs 8:1) are a useful tool for helping pupils to understand how to lengthen their stories. They are designed to work for all learning styles, and it is the kinaesthetic methodology that embeds the process. It is important, therefore, that the activity is done physically in a lively, fun way. When the pupils with the three core blue cards, 'OPENING', 'BODY', 'END' actually move further apart in response to your request for them to 'write a longer story' they see that there are now big spaces that need to be filled.

The filling of those spaces by other pupils holding the content words, ('WHO', 'WHAT', 'WHERE', 'WHY') teaches how to fill those spaces in a piece of writing. This is made fun through the questioning, for example, 'What sort of who are you Mrs. Who?' 'What sort of where are you Mr. Where?' which are usually answered in general terms, for example, 'The main character/s', 'The story setting'. The pupils actually making up a story orally, based round the cards, then reinforce this. The addition of pupils with the 'feelings' words, ('HOPE', 'FEAR', 'THOUGHTS', 'FEELINGS', 'SADNESS', JOY' etcetera) helps the pupils to add detail. These pupils have to say how someone in the story felt. This can be extended by adding description words, ('SCAREY', 'BEAUTIFUL', 'CALM', 'PEACEFUL', 'EMPTY', 'FLAT', 'HILLY' etcetera). These, however, need to be added by selection, to make them appropriate for context, and are effectively taught by scribing them as pupils suggest them, and giving them to the content card holders, as that is where they would be in writing. Pupils should use these cards shortly before writing.

After 'playing' the whole 'game' once or twice, it is usually sufficient to hold up the cards one by one, or pass them out to pupils who remain seated. When all are confident with structure, the cards can be put along the top of the teaching wall, (see 'The Positive Writing Environment'). They then form a prompt or scaffold for pupils' writing as they work.

Actually asking pupils to 'make up' the next line of a story, using their Story Structure Card to inform their sentence, rather like the game 'Consequences', can extend the fun.

> ## Planning writing

Planning writing is a sensitive area. Different learning styles impact on pupils' attitudes to planning. Some pupils do not value planning at all, and find it tedious, which leads to de-motivation before the writing process starts. Other pupils benefit from time invested in planning, but may not equally value the method/s offered in your class.

It is useful to teach pupils several different ways to plan a story, and then to allow them to choose the method they prefer. Make planning a short process, but be flexible at the opening of writing time so that those who wish to can spend a little longer gathering their thoughts.

Alternatively, build planning time into the timetable for the day before the writing day, so that at least pupils' first thoughts are pre-recorded.

The following are some of the ways of planning that work for many pupils:

1. The cartoon strip:

>1.	>2.	>3.
>4.	>5.	>6.

This may have four, six or eight frames depending on age or degree of support needed. Very young pupils and pupils with special educational needs may plan the whole story this way, with help. They may write only with support, then illustrate without help. They may draw the sequence and then insert simple words and phrases. They may draw the sequence and then write the story, with help if required.

> Planning writing

2. The single bubble:

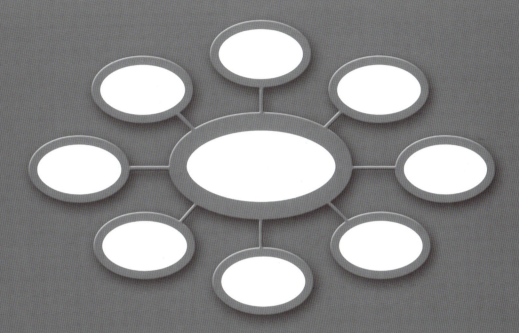

Pupils put the title or the main character in the middle and jot all their first thoughts around it. These may be characters, places, events etcetera. **See Example over page**

3. The mind map:
Single Bubble Planning Model

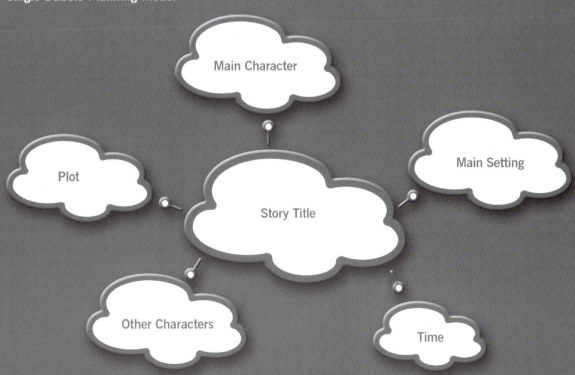

Single Bubble Planning Example

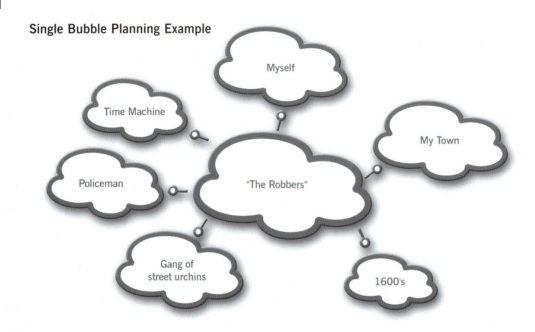

Mind Map Example

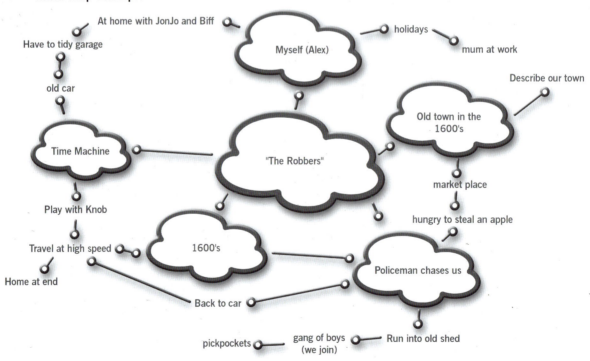

Pupils put the title in the middle and follow their thoughts out in a web like formation based on themes or sequenced events. More engrossing if using coloured pens or pencils. See Network Press publications for mind mapping. **See Example over page**

Planning Writing

4. The traditional scaffold:

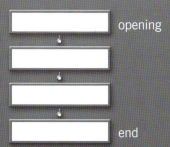

(Series of 4 boxes one above the other with a small space between and an arrow in the space, pointing downwards)

5. Clouds:

(A series of four to six 'thought clouds' Floating on the page. Arrows can then be inserted by the pupil to make links if desired, with notes between.)

6. Lists:
(Pupil has coloured paper and coloured pens or pencils. Lists her / his key thoughts and jots notes around the listed items, draws arrows, makes small sketches etcetera.)

7. Planning partners:
(Oral discussion only in the first instance. Five minutes free talk, then partners decide whether to change to a recorded form or continue discussion)

8. Story Scaffold Cards (See LSMs 8:1):
(Give pupils the teaching SSCs or mini-versions of them. If they are laminated, pupils can make notes on them with whiteboard pens, and slide them around on a table or the floor while planning the main elements of their story. This is best done with a planning partner, or a teaching assistant if the pupil has special educational needs.)

Pupils will show differing attitudes to planning on different days. Allow them to show their individuality through their choice of the method of planning, and if a pupil does not wish to plan one week, encourage them to draw / annotate an illustration of key characters instead, or to collect ambitious words and phrases appropriate to the subject matter using a thesaurus and / or dictionary.

Planning is supposed to be a useful tool. It is not useful if pupils do not value it!

> ## The Positive Writing Ethos

Creating a positive ethos for writing is crucial. **All children need to have high self-esteem and motivation in order to succeed.**

There are five elements that the class teacher can control and influence to create high self-esteem:

1. All children need to work in an atmosphere that is positive.
2. All children need to work in an atmosphere in which they feel secure.
3. All children need to feel in control of their immediate circumstances.
4. All children need to feel successful and valued.
5. All children need to work positively towards goals that they understand and feel are attainable.

Ask yourself;

"DO ALL THE CHILDREN IN YOUR CLASS FEEL LIKE THIS EVERY DAY, IN EVERY LESSON AND IN ALL ASPECTS OF SCHOOL?"

Remember;

YOU MAKE THE DIFFERENCE!

Those of us who work with children who have low self-esteem, need to work all the harder to compensate, and to provide an environment within which these children have the opportunity to feel valued and successful.

Remember:

YOUR SELF-ESTEEM IMPACTS ON THE ETHOS IN YOUR CLASSROOM

The Positive Writing Ethos

THE IMPORTANCE OF TEACHERS' ATTITUDES

Many teachers have had their self-esteem persistently eroded over the last decade and a half, through working in a 'blame' culture where failure of teachers has been seen as the root of many things wrong with young people and society. This climate is now changing and teachers should feel confident to raise their heads and believe in themselves again.

One of the least successful areas in terms of raising standards in national tests, has been the writing strand of English. Although teachers have worked hard to raise standards, lack of a clear understanding of progression in writing skills has often led to energy being misdirected into the range of opportunities to the exclusion of the development of the full range of generic skills, which are transferable across genre.

If the skills of writing are taught systematically, working consistently through a progressive framework of criteria as the pupils move through the school, teachers will be rewarded by measurable success for the majority of pupils, which can be predicted and guaranteed. This needs to take place alongside the teaching of text types through the literacy strategy or the school's English Scheme of Work.
To impact quickly on standards in writing, (or in any other area), teachers themselves need:

* belief that they have the knowledge and understanding essential to teach effectively
* belief in the ability of all children to make progress
* a reliable framework for teaching that gives a proven progressive path through the skills required
* willingness to make change and adapt as new approaches are suggested
* the enthusiasm and energy to implement new or adapted ideas

FIVE ELEMENTS OF A POSITIVE ETHOS

1. CREATING A POSITIVE ATMOSPHERE:

i)   talk about writing as an exciting, empowering skill

ii)   talk about the weekly writing session as a high spot of the week

iii)   build up anticipation through the week, (for this purpose I like to have the writing session on a Thursday if possible)

iv)   constantly praise the whole class and each pupil within the class

v)   make constant references to how successful everyone is in writing, at other points in the week and in front of others

vi)   create opportunities for all children to succeed in some way, every day

vii)   ensure all pupils leave the class at the end of the day feeling good about what has been achieved, and secure about their place in the class

viii) use a lively teaching style and intimate that learning, progress, and writing are fun

2. CREATING A SECURE ATMOSPHERE

i)   never use sarcasm

ii)   never publicly ridicule a pupil

iii)   avoid shouting, except in extreme situations, (remember, the less we shout the more effective it is if we have to do it)

iv)   create an atmosphere of calm and serenity, (many of us believe that the use of soft music and aromas is helpful to promote an atmosphere for concentration)

v)   constantly praise the whole class and each pupil within the class

vi)   ensure that you acknowledge the efforts of every pupil every session, if only by a quiet word or smile

vii)   praise pupils who have not yet shown progress, and make them feel they are moving forward

viii)   create opportunities for all children to succeed in some way, every day

ix)   ensure all pupils leave the class at the end of the day feeling good about what has been achieved, and secure about their place in the class

x)   use an assessment tool that enables you to recognise and celebrate progress in very small steps, (The Criterion Scale does this)

3. CREATING AN ETHOS WITHIN WHICH CHILDREN FEEL IN SOME CONTROL

i)   listen carefully to children when they are talking to you and when they are in discussion with others

ii)   do not assume you are always right, or that your way is the only way

iii)   do not assume that there is only one 'right' answer

iv)   consult children, and involve them in decisions

v)   explain what is happening to children and what you expect the outcome to be

vi)   share teaching objectives with children at the beginning of lessons, in a form they can easily understand, and involve them in meaningful review and evaluation at the end of lessons

vii)   ensure the plenary, and intermediate review points, always include praise and all pupils having a feeling that their efforts have been appreciated

viii)   empower children, by giving them choices whenever feasible

ix)   empower children by giving them responsibilities

x)   SHARE ASSESSMENT PROCESSES AND CRITERIA WITH CHILDREN, IN A WAY THEY CAN UNDERSTAND, AND INVOLVE THEM IN THE PROCESS

> # The Positive Writing Ethos

4. CREATING AN ATMOSPHERE WITHIN WHICH CHILDREN FEEL SUCCESSFUL

i)   ensure children know what success will be measured by

ii)   be aware that there are many other forms of success, and be prepared to be reactive to them

iii) be generous with praise, it costs nothing and means a lot

iv)   talk to children in a positive and cheerful way

v)   develop tangible ways of demonstrating success that all can share in, such as treats at 'story time', grapes while writing, celebrations, and reward systems that all pupils achieve within

vi)   create opportunities for celebration and praise

vii) create opportunities for all children to succeed in some way, every day

viii) ensure all pupils leave the class at the end of the day feeling good about what has been achieved, and secure about their place in the class

ix)   SHARE ASSESSMENT PROCESSES AND CRITERIA WITH CHILDREN, IN A WAY THEY CAN UNDERSTAND, AND INVOLVE THEM IN THE PROCESS

5. CREATING A FRAMEWORK FOR PUPILS TO WORK TOWARDS KNOWN, ACHIEVABLE GOALS

i)   SHARE ASSESSMENT PROCESSES AND CRITERIA WITH CHILDREN, IN A WAY THEY CAN UNDERSTAND, AND INVOLVE THEM IN THE PROCESS

ii)   give children goals that are very close to their current level of achievement, and thus feel within their grasp

iii) talk with children about their work and how it is moving toward the goals

iv)   celebrate children's success as they move towards their goals, or attempt to do so

v)   develop ways that measure children's success and publicly celebrate it, e.g. 'Leading Goal Scorers' poster, (see 'The Writing Environment')

Creating a positive environment for writing will help to embed learning, to raise the status of writing as an activity in your classroom and to motivate pupils.

There are four aspects of the environment that the class teacher can use to create a high profile for writing and to motivate pupils:

6. Use all space round the main teaching point in your classroom, (e.g. the wall round the teaching board) for writing displays. Create 4 areas to promote each of the 4 Generic Targets.
7. Use a display board or similar identified area to celebrate achievement through goals scored.
8. Use gaps in displays, windows etcetera for motivational phrases and spurs to achievement.
9. Provide water for pupils to drink on an ongoing basis.

Ask yourself;

"DO ALL THE CHILDREN IN YOUR CLASS FEEL EXCITED AND EMPOWERED ABOUT WRITING?"

Remember;

YOU MAKE THE DIFFERENCE!

THE EFFORT YOU, (OR A TEACHING ASSISTANT, VOLUNTEER PARENT OR SIMILAR), PUTS INTO THE ENVIRONMENT, IMPACTS ON THE EXCITEMENT ABOUT WRITING IN YOUR CLASSROOM.

PRESENT ALL EXEMPLIFICATION MATERIALS TO A GOOD QUALITY AND LARGE SCALE. THE AMOUNT OF CARE YOU TAKE IN PRESENTATION GIVES SUB-CONSCIOUS MESSAGES ABOUT THE IMPORTANCE OF WORK.

Identify appropriate rewards and incentives for 'practice goals' scored i.e. the answering of quick-fire questions in warm-ups etcetera. E.g. washed grapes, small sweets to be eaten at an agreed time, (subject to school policy) or other rewards.

The Positive Writing Environment
Five Elements of a Positive Environment

6. USE OF THE MAIN TEACHING AREA:

Pupils spend more time looking at the wall behind your main teaching point, than any other. By using this area as a central display area for the VCOP and celebration of achievement you are maximising use of visual impact.

Allocate four points round the main teaching board, (if relevant) to the four features of good writing, (VCOP). You will not need the same amount of space for each of the features.

i)   The Punctuation Area: This will only contain the Punctuation Pyramid
ii) The Openers Area: This will have examples of interesting openers collected during any text work in any lesson, and especially during story and literacy. Some examples will change weekly.
iii) The Connectives Area: This will have examples of interesting connectives collected during any text work in any lesson, and especially during story and literacy. Some additions may be made weekly.
iv) The Vocabulary Area: This will grow and change constantly as new examples of exciting and ambitious vocabulary are found. As words are replaced, they may be moved to the tops and bottoms of other walls.

Make all examples to a high quality and display them well.

Remember:

A   Constantly refer to them in your teaching
B   Play games with them, as exemplified in the lesson notes and Lesson Support Materials notes.
C   Ask pupils to close their eyes and recall what is within a specific area

THIS WILL EMBED THE EXAMPLES IN PUPILS' MINDS SO THAT THEY WILL BE THERE TO SUPPORT THEM AT FUTURE POINTS WHEN THE WALL HAS BEEN CHANGED OR CANNOT BE SEEN.

7. THE 'CELEBRATING ACHIEVEMENT' BOARD

This will preferably be on the main teaching wall to one side of the main teaching point. It should at least be clearly visible and well maintained. (See exemplar photographs in 'St. Matthew's Primary School Case Study').

The main heading should be something motivating, e.g. 'Scoring Goals in Writing', 'Write on Target' or 'Team X League Table' (name of class inserted for X)

This board will contain:

i) The 'Team X League Table' poster. This will preferably be A1 in size. It will be made to a high standard and will have columns to record names of pupils as they move up a sub-level. The columns will be headed, 'One Goal', 'Two Goals', 'Three Goals', 'Four Goals' and 'Five Goals'. All pupils' names start in the 'One Goal' column at the start of the year. They are told this is a celebration of the standards they brought with them from the previous class. Few pupils will move more then five sub-levels in a year, and if they do they deserve a special, separate celebration! Pupils' names should be processed onto cards, (approximately 60 by 100cms) and blu-tacked into the appropriate column. A great fuss should be made when a pupil moves a sub-level, and the name card is moved along a column.

NB – THE COLUMNS DO NOT RELATE TO N.C. LEVELS AND ALL PUPILS HAVE EQUAL OPPORTUNITIES TO MOVE SUB-LEVELS AT THE LEVEL THEY ARE WORKING. HOWEVER, DO PROTECT PUPILS WHO ARE MOVING MUCH SLOWER THAN THE MAJORITY BY FINDING SMALL STEPS FOR THEIR PROGRESS. ALSO, WARN PUPILS THAT SOME STEPS TAKE LONGER THAN OTHERS, AND GIVE AN INDIVIDUAL A QUIET REMINDER OF THIS IF THEY ARE STATIONARY FOR A LONG TIME. IDENTIFY SMALL STEPS THROUGH THE NUMBER OF BULLETS ACHIEVED AS AN ALTERNATIVE CELEBRATION.

ii) Generic Targets for the whole class, extracted from the main pitch within the Four Generic Targets or The Criterion Scale

iii) The listed 'Leading Goal Scorers' A4 sheet each week, giving excerpts that scored goals for class members. (see LSM 4:1)

iv) The 'Leading Goal Scorers' laminated card or white board, (may need to be above / below / at the side of the celebration board). This will also have columns for the number of goals scored, and these are written on with whiteboard marker weekly, each time the pupil scores an important goal during the week. E.g. the 'Leading Goal scorers' for excerpts names go on for one goal, pupils who use a displayed ambitious word without being prompted score one goal, pupils who bring in an exciting example from home score one goal, etcetera. You make the decisions.

v) May display examples of pupils' writing from recent weeks

8. USE OF GAPS IN DISPLAYS / WINDOWS ETCETERA
Use every space to display well-made examples, captions and slogans to motivate pupils. Make them visually stimulating and refer to them in teaching. Change them regularly and ask, 'What's new?' First to spot scores a goal!
i) Use to relocate important examples from main teaching wall as new ones are generated
ii) Use for captions such as 'Write on Target', 'Top Team!' and 'Golden Goals'
iii) Use for motivating slogans such as, 'Up-level / Levels Up!' and 'Write Right!'

The Positive Writing Environment
Opportunities for the four generic targets

YOUR PUPILS WILL ENJOY MAKING UP EXAMPLES OF CAPTIONS AND SLOGANS FOR THE WALLS!

REMEMBER – DISCUSS ALL DISPLAYS WITH PUPILS, AND USE THEM IN YOUR TEACHING.

9. PROVIDE WATER FOR PUPILS

Everyone benefits from having constant access to drinking water. This need not be the hazard many teachers fear.

Sealed water bottles with permanent drinking tubes are readily available, and in most schools pupils can be expected to wash and fill their own bottles. Older pupils will enjoy the responsibility of helping younger pupils with this in lunch times or after school. Alternatively, pupils can be expected to take them home each evening, empty, for washing.

Every bottle should be clearly named with permanent marker.

Water fountains could be provided for filling water bottles, in highly visible public areas. In most schools pupils will quickly learn to fill their bottles in their own time.

In a small number of schools teaching assistants or lunch time supervisors may be given additional responsibilities such as washing the water bottles on a rota basis.

Many schools provide containers in the centre of blocks of desks, or on locker tops, to store water bottles when not in use.

After the initial novelty pupils soon settle into using water bottles in a sensible manner, and at sensible intervals.

10. PROVIDE A WRITING PORTFOLIO FOR PUPILS THAT IS SIGNIFICANTLY 'BETTER' THAN THEIR USUAL FILES/BOOKS.

For example a display album with plastic pockets into which the writing can be inserted. A ten-pocket album will hold twenty pieces of writing back-to-back. It can be taken out at the end of each term and stapled into a writing booklet. Pupils will enjoy designing their own covers and the album can be reused the next term. Also provide a special pen or pencil and any other materials that will make the writing session significant.

St. Matthew's CE. Primary School

Val. Walsh taught a class of 35 Year 4/5 mixed-age pupils for literacy, in an inner-city primary school in Yorkshire in the academic year 2001 to 2002. She taught Literacy/English to three different classes.

Following input on 'Raising Standards in Writing' at an EAZ network meeting, Val decided to create the positive writing environment. The following are excerpts from the notes, and photographic illustrations sent to me by Val. as an outcome of this work.

'I use the punctuation levels at the beginning of every piece of extended writing, in order to remind the children what they are aiming for. I usually write a couple of sentences on the board, minus punctuation, and ask the children to identify which punctuation marks are needed, using their punctuation fans to show me the missing marks.'

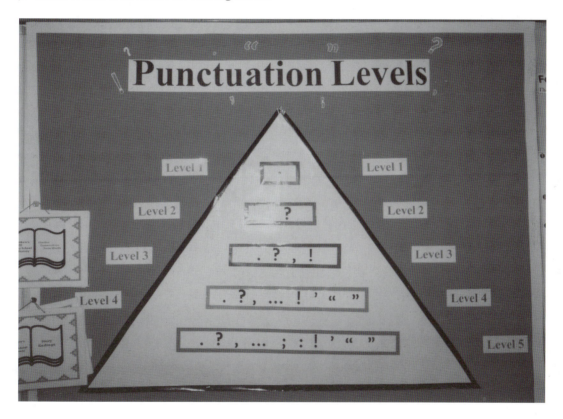

Val's version of the Punctuation Pyramid

'I also put small cards on each table, (you can just see them hanging up in bags underneath the triangle) to remind children which level they are aiming for. They all know where they are, and someone working generally within Level 3 will be given a Level 4 card. I also do as you suggested, and stop the children at intervals to ask them how many different punctuation marks they have used.'

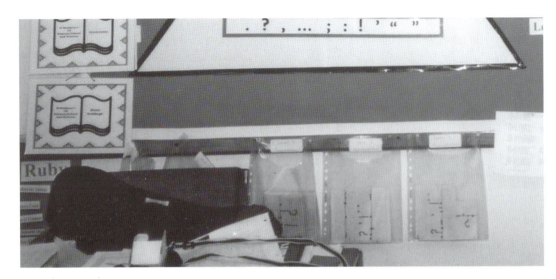

Val's ' Level Cards' hang in bags ready for use.

At the beginning of the school year I assess their writing and give the children a level, e.g. 2a. We formally assess three times a year after this and a child scores a goal if they move a sub-level, e.g. to 3c. I have found that some children appear to go backwards or under-perform at times, but I do not move anyone backwards and they always seem to 'bounce back' after a quiet word pointing out what is happening. In addition, I only move a child one goal at a time, even if their work on a given occasion is very much better than previously. I am finding that at the higher levels of 4 and 5, children are less likely to move more than two sub-levels and thus they have less chance of scoring goals. I am considering awarding these children goals if they achieve the three targets I set for them, even if this does not result in a sub-level move.'

Val's version of the 'League Table' with pupils' names recorded on the footballs. A pupil's ball moves up a level when s/he moves a sub-level in writing.

'These displays and resources have promoted lots of interest, and have increased the children's motivation. To any 'doubters', the plus side of this permanent display is that it cuts down on the need to be endlessly changing this wall!'

> Next
High Crags
Case study

Strategies for Immediate Impact on Writing Standards

> **The Positive Writing Environment**
Case Studies

High Crags
Primary School

> ## The Positive Writing Environment
> ## Case Studies cont

This case study exemplifies good practice in creating the climate for success through a positive ethos for writing. It also contains exemplification materials for two pupils, Charlotte and Curtis. (Names have been changed for protection).

Exemplification Materials:

Curtis's writing has had the assessments removed and may be used by teachers wishing to standardise their assessment using the Criterion Scale, by assessing each piece of writing and comparing their judgements with those given separately at the end of the section.

Furthermore, one piece of Curtis's work exemplifies the influence text type may have on standards. Curtis needs to be shown this effect and helped to find ways to build the VCOP into the text whatever the subject matter.

The use of a letter form for assessment is one I particularly recommend. It gives a consistency to progression that can be very varied if the context is changed for each assessment. It is possible to be creative with the stimulus of the letter in order to interest pupils and include other text types. For example, the letter could be to or from a famous footballer or pop singer, to Father Christmas or to a pen friend in another country. A particularly popular strategy I use is the series of letters between two fictitious friends from a school of magic, stimulated by the Harry Potter stories.

These include different types of text within the body of the letter. (See LSMs 7:1, 7:2 and 7:3)

HIGH CRAGS PRIMARY SCHOOL - BACKGROUND TO THE CASE STUDY

I first visited High Crags Primary School in September 2001, when I provided staff in-service training on raising standards in writing. The school was in the middle of a major building project, and had been in serious weaknesses since 1997. Free school meals were 32%. The school had undergone significant changes in terms of management, (there were a new Head Teacher, a new Deputy Head Teacher and other new members on the Senior Management Team), and had been re-organised from a First School to a Primary School. The majority of the pupils in this school live in rented accommodation, and the area is identified as an Education Action Zone.

As part of the support I provided for the school, I assessed the unsupported writing of every pupil from Reception to Year 6 and set up a portfolio of assessed work, including targets, spreadsheets and graphs, (as described in my earlier publication, 'Raising Standards in Writing', 2002).

During a recent visit to second-assess pupils' writing in support of the teachers at the school, (in order to confirm their assessments and to identify any areas requiring further support) it became clear that the staff had worked hard to raise standards. They had incorporated many of the strategies recommended during the training into their teaching, particularly the quick impact strategies. Assessment of samples of high, medium and low level pieces of writing showed some remarkable results. Two samples of work from a Year 2 class follow, plus notes on how the class has responded to the initiative.

'BIG WRITING DAY'

June Brown teaches a Year 2 upper set in High Crags Primary School. She is one of a talented team of teachers in this school, who have all worked hard to address the difficulties many of their pupils experience in writing. Following INSET one year ago, initiated by the East Shipley Education Action Zone, all staff have adopted the strategies recommended. In the year 2002 tests and tasks for Key Stage 1, High Crags Primary School has achieved 6% at Level 3, where previously they had none, and have more than doubled the percentage of pupils at Level 2B and above.

June established Friday morning as 'Big Writing Day'. Throughout the week her teaching in all text and word level work is, in her words, 'geared towards Big Writing Day', whilst still addressing the full National Literacy Strategy objectives.

On Thursdays, June gives her pupils the learning objectives for 'Big Writing Day', and time is provided for pupils to develop a plan. For example, the week I visited the objectives were 'To use interesting openers' and 'To use three words to make work more interesting'. The planning time had been used to compose several relevant sentences with interesting openers, and to build a word bank of relevant 'interesting' words. As pupils wrote on 'Big Writing Day', she periodically asked them whether they had used their planned sentences and interesting words, and rewarded them with 'smiley faces' as they did. (June has a range of strategies and formats for planning, and changes them frequently to maintain interest. All writing is always for a clearly identified audience.)

June's pupils receive special pencils, yellow writing paper and line guides on 'Big Writing Day'. These resources are kept for this purpose alone. They have Writing Folders, (the display albums recommended in this publication) in which to store their work. Every pupil has their personal writing targets recorded and stored in their Writing Folder. June circulates while her pupils work, referring them to their targets and giving praise.

The work produced on 'Big Writing Day' is ALWAYS marked over the weekend, and returned to pupils for filing in their Writing Portfolios on Monday mornings.

June marks with reference to the pupils' targets, and gives written and oral feedback against the targets. She adjusts their targets each half term. June uses small sweets as incentives and rewards on 'Big Writing Day' (only), with the permission of the school and parents. Pupils receive them as instant rewards, and all pupils receive three to eat at their leisure as they actually produce their unsupported writing.

June's pupils are filled with excitement as 'Big Writing Day' approaches. She reports that they 'line up before school on Fridays buzzing, saying "It's 'Big Writing Day' today." They have changed attitudes towards writing and are so excited. On Mondays they can't wait to see how they did the week before.'

Teachers from other schools regularly watch June teach literacy. She reports that when they see the standard of work her pupils produce in writing, they are amazed and ask how she does it. She tells them that she uses the strategies from 'Raising Standards in Writing', and particularly the Four Generic Targets and the Punctuation Pyramid.

When I visited June's classroom, the whiteboard at the main teaching point was surrounded by interesting and ambitious words found and used by the children. The following are a range of the words I recorded in this Year 2 classroom:

interaction	magnificent	perched	shocked	mechanism
tormented	delicate	frowned	tempt	horrified
quick-witted				

June reports that as she became increasingly pro-active in teaching to the Generic Targets of sentence openers, connectives, punctuation and ambitious vocabulary, so the level of skill in the pupils' writing increased more rapidly. She noted, therefore, that during the summer term of Year 2 her pupils made remarkable progress. Two examples are given below. It should be noted that June uses retell of a story as a useful strategy to model and stimulate writing, however it is recognised that this can give a less secure assessment as pupils directly quote words and phrases. Please note that June's pupils do this, but later work shows that with good teaching they retain the skills and build them into their repertoire.

Pupil 1   Charlotte S_____   (DoB: 02.02.95)
Charlotte is the eldest of three girls in a large, extended family. Charlotte's mother is a lunchtime supervisor at a local secondary school and her father assembles electric fans in a local company. Charlotte is a quiet and hard working pupil with a lot of friends. She likes school, and especially enjoys science. At home she likes '…. going out to 'the club' at night with Nanna and Grandad, playing bingo, buying raffle tickets, listening to the singers and getting back late.'

In Charlotte's work we track her development from Level 2C in September 2001 to Level 3B in July 2002.

The Positive Writing Environment
Case Studies cont

Pupil 2   Curtis B_____ (DoB: 24.11.95)
Curtis is the only child of slightly more mature parents, and is a member of a large extended family. His mother is a lunch time supervisor and his father makes pistons in a local company. Curtis likes playing with Dale, '....especially at Super Heroes and Justice League'. His favourite time of the week in school is Friday because 'It is Big Writing Day'. Curtis hates wet playtimes, '....because they are boring and you fall out with your mates.'

In Curtis's work we track his development from Level 2C in September 2001 to Level 4C in July 2002.

SAMPLES OF CHARLOTTE'S WORK
SAMPLE 1

Dear mrs Roberts in the holidays I Loved my day out to Famingo Land my FravFat Fide at Fam in go Land was the Clowns I haitit it wene I went oh holiday cause it rained.

Judgement: 2C
Short term targets:
• length, detail, description
• accurate sentence structure and punctuation
• openers and connectives

Sample 1. (11.9.01)

> # The Positive Writing Environment
> ## Case Studies cont

SAMPLE 2

Judgement: 2B
Short term targets:
· letter size/shape, legibility
· range of openers and
  connectives
· range of ambitious
  words.

High Crags Primary School
Crag Road
Shipley
Bradford
BD18 3ES
Friday 14th December 2001

Dear Santa

I have been a good girl so for

Christmas please would you bring me a

Potters wheel, game boy advance, some

sweets, a new beautify, a drill, and a candy floss

maker, Harry Potter and the prisoner of uzz cabab books,

A book mark maker and DE FAWLEY

to move house but stay at this scholl

of course. If I guet a Potty's weel I

would make my mum a varsethat is

beautifully decorated.

Love from Charlotte

The Positive Writing Environment
Case Studies cont

SAMPLE 3

Judgement : 2A
Short term targets:
- accurate cursive writing
- range of punctuation
- ambitious vocabulary

High crags Primary
20th march 2002

Sample 3:

Dear Mrs Robets
I'm writing this letter to tell you how I made my pupet first I helped my group to chose a story. Then I Chose a Charector. My story was the four little pigs and my charecter was the fourth Pig. Next I did my desine After that I started to sew. Sewing Was my ~~of the~~ best bit. After I had done the sewing I started to Look at my desine and see What I needed. ~~than~~ After that I stuck all the things I needed on to it. Then I got my stick that was realy axle and diped it in some glue then I put my axle in the hole that I had left ~~Mean while~~ Mean while I started to stuf ~~it~~ it. Then I glued the bottem and now I just have to put on some material
Love from Charlotte

SAMPLE 4

Sample4:

Dear Sarah   Charlotte

I'm writing to tell you all about my
first flight. In the day butterflys flew all
around me and a squiral ran st rate
infront of me on my branch. I got absolutely
fed up of waiting. My mum ~~~~ kept
telling me to go back to sleep but I couldn't
because I was too excited on the ground
I saw a deer and her thorne. In the
air I saw an eagle. When dusk came
a stronigh wind blew so I puffed
out me wings to try ~~to~~ fly but the
wind past away and it was all
puff and nonsense Then my mother woke
up and said "It's time to fly", so I puffed
out my linings sat up strate and slew
and that's how I became a fly by night
                    ~~~~ Love from
                         Blinek

Judgement: 3B   (May wish to leave as 3c because of
Short term targets: implications of retell
· accurate use of cursive writing
· sophisticated openers and connectives
· ambitious words.

SAMPLE 5

Judgement: 3B
Short term targets:
- accurate cursive writing
- range of sophisticated openers and connectives
- ambitious vocabulary

12.7.02
Sample 5:

The magic ring   Charlotte

One bright Saturday afternoon me and my sister's Emily
and Paige were playing on the beach in Morcambie.
My sister Paige said I could have a turn to
kick her football. I kicked the ball, it flew through
the air and landed ..... SPLASH! in the rockpool "Oh
no!" I said "go get it then" Emily said. "ok, ok, I'm going"
I said. When I went to get the ball I saw something
shiney in the rockpool. I carefuly put my hand in and pulled out
a shiney and delicate ring. It was made of solid gold.
When I put the ring on a voice said "what is your
wish madam". "Whow said that?" I said astonishly. "your
ring madam, it's your ring". "My wish is I could
have a boat ride" "ok madam". And with that the ring
came off of my finger and landed in
the sea but instead of floating it sank.
"But how did that happen I said?".

> # The Positive Writing Environment
> ## Case Studies cont

JUDGEMENTS

CHARLOTTE'S WORK
SAMPLE 1:   11.09.01

Level 2: Charlotte can:
- write with meaning in a series of simple sentences
- produce a short section on one idea
- use vocabulary appropriate to what she means to say
- use simple phonic strategies when trying to spell unknown words, e.g. 'fravrat' and 'haitit'
- use the connective 'when'
- write with a confidence that goes beyond a basic 'list' form and shows the beginning of voice
- use connectives other than 'and', e.g. when, because
- use the adjective 'favourite'
- spell common monosyllabic words accurately

Charlotte is beginning to:
- provide detail that adds interest for the reader
- match the organisation to the purpose of writing a letter

Charlotte can not yet:
- control ascenders and descenders in hand writing
- sustain the form long enough to provide secure evidence
- vary the structure of sentences
- use interesting and ambitious words
- use full stops to show sentences
- provide enough evidence to show use of phonetic strategies
- make writing lively and interesting
- link ideas and events
- structure sentences accurately
- use accurate and consistent hand writing
- join her hand writing

Judgement: 2C

Short-term targets:
1. length and detail
2. sentence structure / punctuation
3. openers & connectives

Charlotte is showing the writing skills of a weak sub-level 2C, however there is little length on which to base a judgement, and the teacher would use her knowledge of Charlotte in order to decide whether she is better left at 1A at this time.

JUDGEMENTS

CHARLOTTE'S WORK
SAMPLE 2:   14.12.01

Level 2: Charlotte can:
• write with meaning in a series of simple sentences
• produce a short section on one idea
• use vocabulary appropriate to what she means to say
• use simple phonic strategies when trying to spell unknown words, e.g. 'fravrat' and 'haitit'
• control ascenders and descenders / upper and lower case
• use several connectives
• write with a confidence that shows the beginning of voice
• sustain the form throughout
• provide interesting detail, e.g. what she would do if she had a potter's wheel
• vary the structure of sentences, e.g. opening with 'If…'
• 2C – use sentence punctuation, sometimes accurately (can be counted towards the eight needed to make a 2C but not towards the thirteen needed to make a 2B or above)
• use connectives other than 'and', e.g. but, so, if
• make writing lively and interesting, e.g. through the use of a connective as an opener and through grouping nouns together with commas to sub-divide
• use the adverb 'beautifully'
• spell common monosyllabic words

Charlotte is beginning to:
• use more interesting words, e.g. 'definitely' and 'decorated' although these are not ambitious for a seven year old
• match the organisation to the purpose of writing a letter
• link ideas and events through connectives but is not yet using link words
• join her hand writing

Charlotte can not yet:
• provide enough evidence to show use of phonetic strategies, (the attempted spelling of 'definitely' does not show secure strategies beyond the simple)
• structure all sentences accurately
• use accurate and consistent hand writing

Judgement: 2B

Short-term targets:
1. range of openers and connectives
2. handwriting – legibility
3. ambitious words

JUDGEMENTS

CHARLOTTE'S WORK
SAMPLE 3: 20.03.02

Level 2: Charlotte can:
- write with meaning in a series of simple sentences
- produce a short section on one idea
- use vocabulary appropriate to what she means to say
- use simple phonic strategies when trying to spell unknown words, e.g. 'pupet' and 'stuf'
- control ascenders and descenders / upper and lower case
- use several connectives
- write with a confidence that shows the beginning of voice
- sustain the form throughout
- provide interesting detail, e.g. the detail of how she made the axle
- vary the structure of sentences, e.g. opening with 'After...'
- show awareness of the organisation of a letter form
- use sentence punctuation, mainly accurately
- use phonetically plausible strategies to spell unknown polysyllabic words, e.g. 'character', 'desine'
- use connectives other than 'and', e.g. then, after
- make writing lively and interesting, e.g. through the use of a connective as an opener and through 'started to' and 'now'
- use link words such as 'meanwhile' 'after that' and 'started to'
- spell common monosyllabic words
- use abstract adjectives and adverbs such as 'some' and 'really'
- structure sentences correctly
- use accurate hand writing
- join her hand writing

Charlotte is beginning to:
- use more interesting words, although these are technical words given to her

Judgement: 2A – assess for Level 3
From Level 3, Charlotte only shows secure evidence that she can:
- develop ideas in sequenced sentences
- use the connective, 'After....'
- usually use correct grammatical structures
- use accurate sentence punctuation
- organise the work clearly with a beginning, middle and end
- spell phonetically regular and familiar polysyllabic words

Therefore the judgement is 2A

Short Term Targets:
1. accurate cursive writing
2. range of punctuation
3. ambitious vocabulary

JUDGEMENTS

CHARLOTTE'S WORK
SAMPLE 4:   18.06.02

Level 3: Charlotte Can
• produce work that is organised and clear
• use a range of forms, (letter follows narrative and report form)
• adapt the form to the audience – showing awareness in opening sentence
• use ambitious words for a seven year old, e.g. 'absolutely'
• develop ideas in sequenced sentences
• use a wider range of connectives, e.g. when, because
• use adjectives and adverbs, e.g. 'first', 'absolutely', 'strong'
• use sentence punctuation accurately
• use the letter structure clearly
• experiment with a range of punctuation, e.g. comma, speech marks, apostrophe
• develop the setting
• give interest through detail

Charlotte is beginning to:
• use correct grammar
• adapt the form for purpose
• use cursive writing accurately
• use sentence punctuation accurately
• use adjectives and adverbs but the evidence is not secure, ('strong wind' could be a remembered phrase)
• spell phonetically regular words correctly but makes mistakes
• link ideas in simple ways only
• develop pace

Charlotte cannot yet:
• use generalising words for style

Judgement: 3B,
but weak because of retell implications. The teacher may leave the child as a 3C for a while

Short-term targets:
1. accurate cursive writing
2. sophisticated openers and connectives
3. ambitious words

JUDGEMENTS

CHARLOTTE'S WORK
SAMPLE 5:   12.07.02

Level 3: Charlotte Can
- produce work that is organised and clear
- use a range of forms
- use ambitious words for a seven year old, e.g. 'delicate' 'astonishedly'
- develop ideas in sequenced sentences
- use a wider range of connectives, e.g. when, instead
- usually use correct grammatical structures
- use sentence punctuation accurately
- use a clear story structure
- experiment with a range of punctuation, e.g. comma, speech marks, apostrophe, ellipses
- use adjectives / adverbs / description e.g. 'a shiney and delicate ring'
- spell phonetically regular or common polysyllabic words e.g. 'delicate', 'finger', 'madam'
- give interest through detail, dialogue and description

Charlotte is beginning to:
- adapt form to audience by providing additional information
- adapt the form for purpose
- use cursive writing accurately, but upper case letters are not clearly defined
- link ideas in simple ways only
- develop pace

Charlotte cannot yet:
- use generalising words for style
- develop the characters, setting or feelings and emotions

Judgement: 3B

Short-term targets:
4. accurate cursive writing, upper / lower case
5. range of sophisticated openers and connectives
6. range of ambitious vocabulary

SAMPLES OF CURTIS'S WORK
SAMPLES 1 and 2

To mrs Roberts,
In my holiday, my mum and dad had to go
to work. So my granny took me to her caravan
I made a couple of streches in the soft play and
two of my mates squashed me with the big soft
balls! In the morning I had to go to my
granny's house but... I only had half a day a full day
and then I had to go home.

Sample 2

Dear Santa

Please may I have a Sho-gun transformer because
I just Love action. And do you mind if you give
me a Track 'n' Attack Max Steel, so it can go with my Cycto
bad guy? Oh, and please can I have a Harry Potter
dressing up set, a remote-controle quad, Harry Potter book
of spells, and ... ofcourse, absolatly, a Harry Potter Lego
set because I don't know what Hog warts School of
wichcraft and wizardry Looks like. And I REALLY, really want
a power-ranger battle-booster because (I think you know)
I Love power-rangers Time Force. From Conor Breen (your
greatest fan!)

SAMPLE 3

Sample 3   Curtis

High Craggs Primary
Wednesday 20th March

Dear Mrs Roberts,

We made puppets and this is how. We thought up some
traditional tales and chose a character. I chose the prince
out of Cinderella. We drew designnes of our puppets.
Meanwhile, we then got the equipment that we would need.
Next we practised stitching so that our puppets would
turn out right. Then it was time to do the real thing!
After that we sewed the front and the back of the head
together. Then we added some facial features. Now we had
to stuff our puppets! We spread some glue onto an old
ruler each. Miss Burns shoved the ruler up our puppets neck.
Everybody put a toilet roll tube up the ruler. Then it was
time to put the clothes on. I chose an red cloak with seagulls
on. Everyone used paperclips to fix the clothes to the toilet
roll tube. Finally, we put a collar round the paperclips to hide
them from view. Our puppets are fishished.

                    Love from Curtis

SAMPLE 4

Sample 4

First oak tree on your right
Owl town
Hadley

Dear Sarah   I am writing this letter to tell you about my first flight. So, here goes. Me and my owl mother were sleeping on our branch. A while later, I woke up. "Is it time yet?" I asked my owl mother. "Soon said my mother. "Go back to sleep". Just when I was watching a weasel scurry past, I heard a voice. It was the wind. "Time to fly" it seemed to whisper as it drifted past me. I knew it was all puff and nonsense. I kept muttering it under my breath. "Time to fly" said my owl mother so I spread out my wings and ..... up, up and away I went! Further and further over a winding river and a road. My first flight a fly by night.

Love from

Blink

SAMPLE 5

Curtis

Sample 5

Rockpools and rings.

Once I was walking along Filey beach. Suddenly, I tripped over a rock and went toppling into the nearest rockpool. "OUCH!" I exclaimed as I stood on something sharp in the water. As I picked up the sharp object, I noticed it was a DIAMOND RING! Because I had stood on the ring I had a scar on the sole of my foot. Meanwhile, my mum and dad took me to the downtown library. As I flicked through the parchment pages of the book I noticed the title. It was Medieval Curses. "The ring of Clion belongs to the wish God Zanzius" I read. "Weird name!" I muttered under my breath. After that, I was using some of the ring's power to make me fly. Amazingly, I saw Zanzius sunbathing on a cloud. "Hey what the." I didn't get to finish my sentence because I fell. I fell through the air. "Ouch" said an old woman as I landed on top of her. Later on, I was playing catch with my ring. If I dropped the ring, it would knock me over with it's powers! But then, I threw the ring too high and Zanzius the wish God caught it, "Oh bother." I muttered.

JUDGEMENTS

CURTIS'S WORK
SAMPLE 1 : 11.09.01

Level 2: Curtis can:
• write with meaning in a series of simple sentences
• develop an idea in one section
• use vocabulary appropriate to the sense of what he wants to say
• has not needed simple phonic strategies as his spelling of regular words is accurate
• can use connectives, e.g. 'and' 'but'
• write more confidently than a basic list form
• provide detail to give interest
• use basic sentence punctuation
• can use the connective 'but'
• use phrases of time to create links
• use adjectives, e.g. 'big', 'soft', 'full'
• usually structure basic sentences correctly
• spell common monosyllabic words accurately

Curtis is beginning to:
• control ascenders but some descenders are above the line
• sustain form, but there is not enough text for secure evidence
• vary the structure, e.g. opening 'In the morning....' but in only one way so there is not enough
  secure evidence
• make his writing lively, but there is not enough to judge if he can sustain it
• use consistent handwriting
• show evidence of joining, but it is only certain in one word, 'big'

Curtis cannot yet:
• use vocabulary interesting or ambitious for a seven year old
• organise a letter
• attempt unusual polysyllabic words that require phonetic strategies

Judgement: 2C
– scores 13, enough for a weak 2B but there is not enough length to give a secure assessment of 2B

Short-term targets:
1. length, detail and description
2. range of openers and connectives
3. ambitious words

JUDGEMENTS

CURTIS'S WORK
SAMPLE 2:   14.12.01

Level 2: Curtis can:
- write with meaning in a series of simple sentences
- develop an idea in one section
- use vocabulary appropriate to the sense of what he wants to say
- has not needed simple phonic strategies as his spelling of regular words is accurate
- use mainly accurate hand writing
- can use connectives, e.g. 'and'
- communicate ideas confidently
- sustain the letter form
- provide detail to give interest
- vary the structure of sentences, e.g. opening with an exclamation and using brackets
- use basic sentence punctuation
- spell complex polysyllabic words mainly accurately
- can use a range of connectives, e.g. 'and', 'because'
- make his writing lively and interesting
- use adverbs and descriptive phrases, e.g. 'really, really, really want', 'absolutely'
- usually structure basic sentences correctly
- spell common monosyllabic words accurately
- use mainly accurate and consistent hand writing
- begin to evidence joining his handwriting

Curtis cannot yet:
- use vocabulary interesting or ambitious for a seven year old
- organise a letter without the scaffold
- use linking strategies

Judgement: scores 19, assess for Level 3

The Positive Writing Environment
Case Studies cont

Level 3:
Curtis can:
- show a clear beginning and end
- adapt the form to the audience through providing additional information e.g. why he needs the lego set, and through the way he 'talks' with the audience e.g. '…of course, absolutely…..'
- develop and extend ideas
- use the connective 'because'
- usually use correct grammatical structures
- adapt the style for purpose – communicating clearly with a particular person
- experiment with a wider range of punctuation, including ellipses, commas and brackets
- spell phonetically regular polysyllabic words accurately, e.g. 'dressing', 'remote', 'greatest'
- attempt interest and opinion, '(I think you know)' 'And do you mind if …'
- show a developing sense of pace, through varied length of sentences and through the range of punctuation – some used for effect

Curtis is beginning to:
- use interesting vocabulary for a seven year old, e.g. 'absolutely' but it is not secure evidence of ambitious vocabulary
- structure sentences accurately, but needs to understand about the appropriate use of 'and'
- use cursive script, but is not yet consistent and accurate
- use adverbs but the only adjective could be a learned 'title', ('bad guy')
- describe feelings and emotions but not yet in a developed way

Curtis cannot yet:
- organise the letter form independently
- use linking strategies
- use generalising words for style
- demonstrate use of a range of forms appropriately and consistently

Judgement: 3C (10 bullets)

Short-term targets:
1. Letter size / shape, cursive writing
2. accurate use of a range of openers and connectives
3. ambitious vocabulary

JUDGEMENTS

CURTIS'S WORK
SAMPLE 3:   20.03.02

Level 3:
Curtis can:
- organise his work clearly
- use a range of forms, (letter follows narrative and report forms)
- develop and extend ideas logically
- use the connective 'so that'
- usually use correct grammatical structures
- use sentence punctuation accurately
- maintain the style for purpose
- use cursive script accurately and neatly
- spell phonetically regular polysyllabic words accurately, e.g. 'puppets', 'added', 'finally'
- link events, e.g. 'Meanwhile…', 'After that…'
- show a developing sense of pace, through varied length of sentences and through the range of punctuation – some used for effect

Curtis is beginning to:
- use interesting vocabulary for a seven year old, e.g. technical language from design and technology and from literacy, but it is not secure evidence of ambitious vocabulary
- structure his work clearly, but the address is not yet laid out accurately
- use adjectives, ('red', 'real') but the evidence is not secure as they may have been given in the teaching

Curtis cannot yet:
- adapt this letter form to its particular audience
- demonstrate a wider range of punctuation in this form
- create the opportunities for detail and description in this form
- attempt opinion, interest or humour in this form
- use generalising words for style

Judgement: 3B (11 bullets)
but the subject matter restricts the style and it is a weak 3B. The teacher may decide to leave the judgement at 3C for one term.

Short-term targets:
4. range of sophisticated openers and connectives
5. range of punctuation for effect and to sub-divide
6. range of ambitious vocabulary

Strategies for **Immediate Impact** on **Writing Standards**

The Positive Writing Environment
Case Studies cont

JUDGEMENTS

CURTIS'S WORK
SAMPLE 4: 18.06.02

Level 3:
Curtis can:
- organise his work clearly
- use a range of forms, (letter follows narrative and report forms)
- adapt the form to the audience e.g. he is 'talking' to a particular person, '...so, here goes...'
- use vocabulary ambitious for a seven year old e.g. 'scurry', 'drifted'
- develop and extend ideas logically
- use a range of connectives
- usually use correct grammatical structures
- use sentence punctuation accurately
- adapt the style for purpose
- experiment with a range of punctuation e.g. speech marks, comma, ellipses
- use cursive script accurately and neatly
- use adjectives and adverbs, e.g. 'winding', 'first'
- spell phonetically regular polysyllabic words accurately, e.g. 'puppets', 'added', 'finally'
- develop a character and setting
- link events, e.g. 'A while later...', 'Just when...'
- attempt to give opinion, interest and humour, e.g. 'I kept muttering it ....'
- show a developing sense of pace, through varied length of sentences and through the range of punctuation – some used for effect

Curtis is beginning to:
- structure his work clearly, but the address is not yet laid out accurately
- use generalising words, e.g. 'seemed'

Judgement: 17, (3A) must assess for Level 4

> ## The Positive Writing Environment
> ## Case Studies cont

Level 4:

Curtis can:

- write in a lively and coherent style
- use interesting language
- use full stops, question marks and commas accurately
- write in a clear, legible, cursive style
- attempt complex structures, e.g. ' "Time to fly" it seemed to whisper as it drifted past me.'
- Spell unfamiliar regular polysyllabic words accurately e.g. 'muttering'
- Use nouns, pronouns and tenses accurately

Curtis is beginning to:

- use a range of styles but there is not sufficient evidence
- organise ideas but the letter form is insecure
- produce thoughtful and considered writing
- use apostrophes and inverted commas
- select from a range of adventurous vocabulary
- select interesting strategies
- develop ideas in interesting ways

Curtis cannot yet:

- use more sophisticated connectives
- use or attempt paragraphs
- use connectives to give order or emphasis
- advise assertively

Judgement: 4C

Short-term targets:

1. use of paragraphs
2. range of sophisticated openers and connectives
3. range of ambitious vocabulary

JUDGEMENTS

CURTIS'S WORK
SAMPLE 5:   12.07.02

Level 4:
Curtis can:
- write in a lively and coherent style
- use interesting language, e.g. 'flicked' 'parchment' 'weird' 'muttered'
- use full stops, and commas accurately
- write in a clear, neat, legible, cursive style
- produce thoughtful and considered writing through use of explanation and justification
- attempt complex structures through opening sentences with adverbs and connectives
- spell unfamiliar regular polysyllabic words accurately e.g. 'parchment', 'muttered'
- use nouns, pronouns and tenses accurately

Curtis is beginning to:
- use a range of styles but there is not sufficient evidence
- organise ideas but needs to attempt paragraphs
- use sophisticated connectives
- use apostrophes and inverted commas accurately
- select from a range of adventurous vocabulary with some words particularly well chosen
- use connectives to give order or emphasis, e.g. 'If I dropped the ring....'
- select interesting strategies such as use of dialogue and punctuation
- develop ideas in creative and interesting ways

Curtis cannot yet:
- use or attempt paragraphs
- advise assertively

Judgement: 4C

Short-term targets:
1. use of paragraphs
2. range of sophisticated openers and connectives
3. range of ambitious vocabulary

> Next
Usher Street
Case study

Usher Street
Primary School

> ## The Positive Writing Environment
> ## Case Studies cont

CASE STUDY

Usher Street Primary School is an average size primary school close to the centre of the city of Bradford in Yorkshire. It draws its pupils from an area of mainly old, terraced housing and council properties. There are a high percentage of pupils having free school meals and a significant number from single parent families.

The current Head Teacher was appointed to the school in September 2001. Ofsted had placed the school in Serious Weaknesses earlier that year. The Head contracted the writer, (in her capacity as a consultant) to work with the newly appointed Year 6 teacher to raise standards in writing, as it was quickly evident that standards were going to be very low. The class teacher was literacy co-ordinator in her previous school and is confident in the strategy. She and the teaching assistant remained in the classroom during the six impact lessons, (which were also observed by the Year 5 teacher) and skilfully built onto the skills taught in the interim weeks.

Background:

The writer baselined all thirty Year 6 pupils one week before the close of school in December 2001, through assessment of a piece of unsupported writing. The following were the baseline findings:

23 pupils were at Level 2
5 pupils were at Level 3
2 pupils were at Level 4

Left without intervention, but with focused, skilful teaching, it was reasonable to expect that the most optimistic prediction would be that most pupils would improve by two sub-levels in the Spring Term. The national forecast for progress for the majority of pupils in any area is around two sub-levels a year. This would mean 5 pupils, (22%) would attain Level 4 in May 2002 tests.

The consultant forecast that 45% to 50% of pupils would attain Level 4 with intervention.

Teaching commenced on January 10th 2002. It took the form of six lessons two or three weeks apart, with two 50-minute sessions split by the morning break. The first session consisted of briskly paced taught inputs and short activities with very little writing. Making disaffected pupils write more does not raise standards! The second session formed the class's main unsupported writing session for the week, and the target was to achieve forty-five minutes of unsupported writing by test week.

In the first lesson no pupil achieved more than thirty minutes of writing, and most wrote little more than a few lines! Fourteen pupils, (almost fifty percent) were on the school's register for special educational needs. The consultant and class teacher agreed that it was unreasonable to expect the five pupils with extreme needs in language to work without support for this length of time. They remained in the classroom for the first session, but worked in the shared area with the teaching assistant for the second half of the lesson. It is advised that teaching assistants be trained in the VCOP and Level 2 criteria to help them to support pupils in developing independent use of skills.

EVIDENCE BASE FOR THE CASE STUDY

The following pages consist of:
- Spreadsheet to show monthly value added progress for each pupil, culminating with the April assessment. At this point 30% of pupils were at Level 4 and a further six were at a secure or high Level 3. One further lesson then took place and incentives were increased by promising mention in this publication if they did well!

- The final test outcomes for 2002

- Evidence of progress in writing for two pupils. This work has the assessment left on to exemplify the assessment process of ticking criteria that are securely evidenced, putting a dot if there is a little evidence but it is not secure. A cross is used if there is no evidence. It is the dots and crosses that inform the setting of short-term targets. The number of short-term targets set is always three as this is often enough to move the writing up another sub-level. Counting the ticks only gives the score, which is then matched to the thresholds in the assessment box to identify the sub-level achieved.

USHER STREET PRIMARY SCHOOL
WRITING TEST RESULTS FOR MAY 2002 (NATIONAL TESTS)

Level 2	=	0	=	0%
Level 3	=	11	=	37%
Level 4 and above	=	15	=	50%
Level 5	=	8	=	27%

Improvement By Whole Levels
January 2002 to May 2002

N	+ 1 level	+ 2 levels	+ 3 levels
3	16	7	3

HMI conducting a two-day monitoring visit prior in April, to the tests, described the initiative in writing as having a 'positive effect'.

> The Positive Writing Environment
Case Studies cont

Name	Gender	Other	Base-Line Dec. 2001	Target May 2002	Progress Jan. 2001	Progress Feb. 2001	Progress March. 2001	Progress April 2001	Value Added by Sub Level April 2002	Test Result May 2002	Value Added by Level Jan/May
Sana A	F	EAL	3A	4B	4B	3B	5C	5C	+4	5	+2
Danielle B	F		3B	4C	3A	4B	4B	4B	+3	4	+1
Stephanie B	F		2C	2A	3C	2B	Ab	Ab	X	3	+1
Jessica B	F		2A	3B	4C	4B	5C	5C	+7	5	+3
Gemma B	F		2C	2A	2B	2B	2B	2B	+1	3	+1
Carly C	F		2A	3B	3B	3C	3B	3B	+2	4	+2
Sophie C	F		2B	3C	Ab	Ab	3C	3C	+2	3	+1
Andrew C	M	*	2C	2A	Ab	Ab	2B	2B	+1	3	+1
Nicole D	F	*	2B	3C	2B	2B	2B	2B	=	3	+1
Teri D	F		2B	3C	3B	4C	3B	3B	+3	5	+3
Shauna G	F		2C	2A	Ab	2A	2B	2B	+1	3	+1
Danny G	M	*	2C	2A	2A	1A	2C	2C	=	N	N
Weiling H	F	EAL	3C	3A	3B	3A	4B	4B	+4	5	+2
Shamim H	F	EAL	2C	2A	Ab	2B	2B	2B	+1	3	+1
Ashley J	M		3A	4B	4B	4A	4A	4A	+3	5	+2
Bilal L	M	EAL	2C	2A	Ab	Ab	Ab	2B	+1	3	+1
Adam M	M		3C	3A	4C	3B	4B	4B	+4	4	+1
Benita N	F	EAL	4C	4A	3B	3A	Ab	Ab	X	5	+1
Sarah N	F		3A	4B	3C	3C	3B	3B	-1	4	+1
Jojo O	M		2B	3C	2B	2B	2C	2C	-1	3	+1
Alan P	M	*	2C	2A	2B	2B	2C	2C	=	N	N
Daniel R	M		2A	3B	3C	3B	2B	2B	-1	4	+2
Zeshan S	M	EAL	2B	3C	3B	3B	3C	3C	+2	4	+2
Rachel S	F		4C	4A	4B	4B	4A	4A	+2	5	+1
Brian S	M	*	2C	2A	2C	2B	2C	2C	=	N	N
Jamie S	M	*	2A	3B	3C	2B	2C	2C	-2	3	+1
Danny W	M		2C	2A	2B	3B	3A	3A	+5	4	+2
Umran Y	M	EAL	2A	3B	4B	3B	3A	3B	+2	5	+3
Laura M	F		2A	3B	2B	3B	3B	3B	+2	3	+1

Exemplar 1: Weiling progresses from Level 3C in December to Level 4B in April and attains Level 5 in the national test in May 2002. Value added progress = 2 levels

Sample 1 - Weiling

> Weiling Ho
>
> Thursday 9th January 2002
> Scoring gols in writing
> Using featues in writing "better"
>
> He climed carefully along one of the branches, holding tight to his broomstick, trying to see through the leaves he saw Snape talking to someone and he said "Yes everything is planed out right". It was one of the children in the school, Harry listned as Snape talked Harry listend carefully to what they said. Harry flew back to the school and told them what was going on.
>
> →4   Targets:-
> · accurate senterce structure + punchation
> · range of sentence openers + connectives
> · ambitious vocabulary

Sample 2 - Weiling

Weiling Ho   Wednesday 17th January 2002

THE MONSTER

With fear and dread I crept cautiously down the dark, damp tunnel. My hands were my eyes, nervously seeking the way by tracing the slime covered granite walls. Though I strained to hear and see, there was nothing….. nothing but the sounds of my own strained breathing and the soft pad of my rubber-soled shoes.

Suddenly an evil odour invaded my nostrils, like the rotting filth of a thousand corpses. I stopped, heart pounding. Was something there in the dreaded darkness? No longer able to stand not knowing, I pulled out my flashlight and switched on its harsh beam to light up the tunnel ahead.

Silence, heavy and still, surrounded me. Reassured, I began to step forward… Out of the black depths came a sudden blood curdling howl as the great beast leapt towards me. There, pinned in the beam of my flashlight, I finally saw it….

~~the~~ it had ~~was~~ big large visius fangs it was like a snake but seemed twice as biger than that. Meanwhile I was standing very still like a statue i… i… it was coming towards me. slowly it came then it said.

"Well well well anothe human what are you doing hear?"
"I… I… I… I don't know I forgot" The monster said
"Oh another one forgot. hhh."

(3B) · accurate sentence structure & punctuation
· grammatical structures
· range of operative connectives

Sample 2 – Weiling (cont)

"A
" are you going to e-e...e...ēt me. "
" I'v cours not" the monster replied
Y...Y...Your not.
"What ~~would~~ are
you going to do then."
As they talked, the minits past
and they didn't know that it
was getting darker and darker and
darker.
  Suddenly I felt that someone was coming...another monster
it was the monsters dad the
monsters evil dad.....

Sample 3 – Weiling

Weiling Ho   20.2.02.

(3A) Targets:
- Vary sentence length.
- sophisticated openers & connectives
- ambitious vocabulary

The Cuboard under the
Stairs 4, Privet Drive,
Bradford
20th February 2002

Dear Hermione,

    Thanks for your letter. Do you realy want to know what happend? OK well I was minding my own buisness, when I saw Dumbledore and professor on the top of the tower. Then I thought to my self that I will go up the the top of the tower on my broom stick to find out what is going on. I flew up amediatly I said, "what is going on Mr Dumbledore?"

"I...I...I look behinde you Harry." Then I did I saw the evil bat-winged demon. He had sharp fisouse fangs and red eyes the wings were huge. Dumbledore me and professor was standing very still. Apter a while everyone came of of Hogworts and looked up at us they didn't see the horride bat, because it was small and not tall like us. I didn't push professor you got to beleve me. Do you beleve me? I said to the bat "what do you want and why are you here?"

Sample 4 – Weiling

(4B) ~~Thursday 21st March 2002~~ Weiling
You're in charge

Targets:
• menage time to complete work
• spelling strategies
• accurate use of punctuation; including ?

"Bring bring" the telephone rang "Hello Michelle speaking." I said pollitety.
"Oh hellow Michelle I was wondering if you can come tonight to babysit our baby."
"Of corse I will. ~~Okay~~ I'll come now bye. ✱" I rushed to the house and knoked on the door "knok knok."
"Oh hear allready. Well you'v better come in then," As soon as Louises mum and dad left the house Louis rushed to her room, she was only a baby and she was cute. I follo wed her. She kept looking at a ~~vers~~ varse, I toched it and looked inside it
~~Suddenly~~ Suddenly I saw a flash I closed my eyes then opened it again......I was in a nother place a nother country ~~or~~ or may be a nother world in sted. There was lots of trees and sand on the ground, then I thought to my self, how am I going to get out of hear? Although I was in a nother place I was thinking ✱ was I in the past ~~of~~ or future even, ~~no~~ I wouldn't be in the future. I felt the leaves on the trees "oaw. thougs are leathal ~~aret~~ aren't they.
"Louise ~~where~~ where are you going."

Sample 4 – Weiling (cont)

"gu gue" it said "ohhh" I followed...a...a...a...a...a animal w...w...
with a humans head and, a body of a
lion and, a tail of a cat," what is
that thing called?" I said
                "Hello" it said in a ~~low~~
low voice.
"D..d...d...~~don't~~ don't eat me or the
baby!" I shouted at it. "I won't eat
you why would I."
"Y...y...y... you'r not going to
eat me." It showed me the way to
go home but he said" ~~e~~ First you have
to pass this test." I had to go into
a tree. A queastion came on it. It
said what would you want best
a D.V.D. or to look after the baby. I
didn't know what to chose I chose the
baby. A big flash came, and

Sample 5 – Weiling

(3A) Togats:
· accurate grammatical structures ire of punctuation including ? · accurate use of punctuation range of sophisticated vocabulary

Weiling Ho Thursday 2nd May 2002
It wasn't meant to end like that.

"Claire you can't... you just can't."
I shouted to Claire on the phone.
"But why not they don't even cer about me, there leving with out mo m, she replide.
"Why don't you stay hear until the get back. I said.
"But... oh all right I too won't crash the my perants car then."
I said "well you haven't got, yo driving licence yet haven't you.
"No I guess ques not." Clair said upsetly, Meanwhile chelsea & was waching T.V. "Chelsea why don't you just get your make up on or somethi g" I yelled at her. "Oh all right.
'Ding dong,' It was Claire. "Oh hello c laire come in.." I said cheareully.
"So where's my room, then..
"you don't have a room, you may have to sleep on the sopher. I replide.
"I'm not sleeping there." She shouted
"I'm going out" Claire so shouted cross ly. "Stam." She slamed the door, 'BANE
Claire was driving her perants car She was upset about her perants leaving her, that she was crying. Claire wasn good at driving a car. Then suddenly it happened 'CRASH'. The ambulance came
"What happened" I shouted to the pec

Sample 5 – Weiling (cont)

Weiling Ho

There was a huge crowd. "excus me
do you know this woman." A person
said to me he was driving the Ambulan
e. "Yes she's my freind." I cryed.
"where's her perants she's there on h-
oliday." "Is she going to be alright." I
said. "Don't worry she's in safe hands
now." The man said. "It wasn't meant to end like that." I cryed. "what
are we going to do?" I went to hospital
with ther and chelsea too I was
going to ring Claires perants but one
problem... I didn't know there phone num
ber. Claire had to stay in hospital for
3 weeks she was okay then. Claire had
to come home, well in plat until
her perants come back but it was
alright.
"Claire toast is ready, shall
I bring it up."
"Yes thank you." Claires parents
came back and never igroured her again.

Exemplar 2: Danny progresses from Level 2C in December to Level 3B in April, and attains Level 4 in the national test in May 2002. Value added progress = 2 levels.

Sample 1 – Danny

Thursday 10th January   NAME Danny Ward

Scoring Goals in Writing
• using features to write "better"

Harry tried two bee trous the bushes, Harry tried to look put his foot but foot sliped and his body fell out of the tree. Snape saw Harry and run off into the distance. Harry saw quirrel, quirrel said, Stop! said harry I never heared everthing but I hearded enough.

Targets:-
 · adjechives / aduerbs
 · rage of operes & connechives
 · ambitious vocabulary

Sample 2 – Danny

Danny Ward   17.1.02

THE MONSTER

With fear and dread I crept cautiously down the dark, damp tunnel. My hands were my eyes, nervously seeking the way by tracing the slime covered granite walls. Though I strained to hear and see, there was nothing..... nothing but the sounds of my own strained breathing and the soft pad of my rubber-soled shoes.

Suddenly an evil odour invaded my nostrils, like the rotting filth of a thousand corpses. I stopped, heart pounding. Was something there in the dreaded darkness? No longer able to stand not knowing, I pulled out my flashlight and switched on its harsh beam to light up the tunnel ahead.

Silence, heavy and still, surrounded me. Reassured, I began to step forward... Out of the black depths came a sudden blood curdling howl as the great beast leapt towards me. There, pinned in the beam of my flashlight, I finally saw it....

A blood sucking, vomiting, ugly drastic beast, with big broutly face, fitting fangs drooping, blood fangs fearsly it was. I said ahhh! but instead of running I played music.... th... th... the monster he went asleep or shund I say the big red eyed ugly bear went asleep.

Before and after I past the brutaly beast I just ran from the beast I could see a light I ran, ran and ran even more, but then....... I saw..... I saw a ciclops I tried to sneak past him puck me up

Sample 3 – Danny

Wednesday, 26th February 2002   Danny Ward

(3B) Targets:

· accurate sentence structure + punctuation

· grammatical structures

· range of openers + connectives

The cupboard
under the stairs,
4, privet Drive,
Bradford
20th of February
2002

Dear
Hermione,

Thank you for you're letter, I'M sorry
to say but it's true I have been expelled because everyone
that was
on the ground says that, I pushed him on
the roof to the ground and he says a diffrent
story all together. He says a dimon pushed him
off and Just to make it clear I did not
push him off at all OK?. I was Just getting
on to the roof I know I never but for
all you know the demon could of transformed
into me because Dumbledore said that look like me
but when he first saw it he said it looked
like this bloody python fang a terrible stench
but or some sort of using dooeply dragon
feet webed feet also he said. Astonishly flash
demon put him up flews off the building
and droped him.
Just   so you know he is in proving.

P.S
Hermione I've got to start this out However
I do it don't worry

you're sincerely
yours friend Harry

Sample 4 – Danny

Thursday 21st March 02   Danny ward

(3A →)

Targets: URGENT
• accurate sentence
  structure / punctuation
• grammatical structures
• proof read

**You're in
charge**

1 para   Although my mission is to save
Eghipt!....I need this special cross, which is a
Key, to go in the caves to stop the earth-
quake from making the volcano from erupting
anxiously I went and to the inder-
ground the time was 7:15. I was
dripping from head to toe with sweat,
It was so dark that I had ten
matches altogether.

2 para   I got in, out, swipt my guns,
no one was their. Until I could sences
someone behind me. I swiftly turned
around and started to shoot bam bam
bam. The robotic tiger that had
eyes like a demon, was compltly
shaterd, I opend it up got the cross
Known as the cross of Jesus got
it and got back down the
tunnel before the tomb colapst it
colapst becaus it was very old
and had no standing poles.

3 para   I rushed back down the tunnel
and got back out,
got in the 4x4 Jeep and rushed
up the mountain fully speed.
Jumpt out of the 4x4 Jeep and
for got to put the hand break
and it went tumbeling back down
down the mountain.

Sample 5 – Danny

Danny Thursday 2nd May 02,
Ward   It wasn't ment
(3B) Targers: to end like that......
• accurate sentence structure,
  punctuation / capitals
• range of openers / connectives
• clarify through explanation

10:30 AM I got up. church was on my
mind. I got drest and got into my
car a drove off. I got to church
but on the door it said
CLOSED. I looked at my watch,
and it said 10:35AM. So I just
walked in (cus), I remembered
that I put the sign on last night,
so I took it and put it in back
boot in my car I locked my car up
and walked bback in the church,
the church was emty, the vicor
said John .... John people musnt
like my preaching no more? I don't
no people has been talking
about you in the vilgee but
I still like you reaching goods
great life.
I came back out of the church
and went to the shop to pick
up a few things but the
I sore on the foot path
a foot ball. I jumpt out grabed
it and flung it in the back
went carry ing on to the shop.
anny how I got to the shop and
saw a few spuder and bangers
and stink boms and fart spray
and best of all cap guns.

Sample 5 (part 2) – Danny

So went to the resterant
with the goodies   I'll I Set
off the some of the stinking bones
and then the fart spray and
then the spiders I let loose
on the floor.
I scared the living day light out of
them.
then I wen on the motoway
bridges and let the cap guns
Off it never done nothing
So I puct up rocks and stone
and... and... and throw them, them
all it coursed crashes it caused
havoc So I shouted It wasn't
ment to end like that...

Six Lessons for Quick Impact

These lessons are not standard lessons. They are designed for Upper Key Stage 2 pupils and should be modified for younger pupils. They were planned to be taught in two fifty-minute sessions, ideally straddling a playtime within the same morning. This requires a timetable adjustment to accommodate the majority of one morning being dedicated to raising standards in writing. The session could incorporate the time normally dedicated to Literacy Hour, and the additional time required for extended writing.

These lessons are not necessarily to be taught over consecutive weeks. For classes that have a great deal of progress to make, they are better taught at two to three week intervals, with additional opportunity for consolidation built into the interim weeks. All the short activities and taught inputs can be re-planned and taught with small changes to maintain interest.

Each session is presented in two forms, as standard lesson plans and as Lesson Plan Notes. Lesson Support Materials, (LSMs), are referenced in the Lesson Plans and Notes, and exemplified in the third section, with additional supporting notes on how they may be used.

ALL LESSON PLANS ARE INTENDED TO BE ADAPTED AND ADJUSTED TO SUIT THE NEEDS OF YOUR PARTICULAR PUPILS.

EXEMPLAR MATERIALS – EDIT FOR USE

Subject: English Writing
Class: KS2
Date: Week 1

KEY OBJECTIVE: to recognise and use the four generic targets

Objective	Activity	Differentiation	Resources	Evaluation
1. Can we show what we know about punctuation and connectives?	**Warm up: (15 mins.)** Range of punctuation –children name / you record on board. (Do not add to theirs). Ask volunteers to come out and illustrate examples named. Connectives…. Children name / you record on board. If do not recognise term, try 'joining words' and if needed, give 'and' as example. If no recognition, plan taught input on connectives / increase opportunities for recognition in text level work, (TLW) and story. Activity: Give several pairs of sentences asking pupils to record the connective they would use on a white board OR to use a connectives fan to show and say. Record key objective and discuss.	Group / adult support & by outcome (Individuals may have had brief input to prepare them, so are able to make a contribution, or may have LSA softly supporting)	LSM 8:4 Punctuation Pyramid	
2. Can we identify features that show higher levels in writing?	**Taught: (15 mins)** OHP: Excerpt from Harry Potter … in 2s; 'Spot the Differences'…. Discuss what makes second excerpt a 'higher level' than first. Identify range of punctuation, and connectives if able. Steer towards sentence openers and vocabulary. Use to establish idea that there are ways of improving 4 features of writing that will make their writing a higher level. Introduce Punctuation Pyramid. What do they think it means? Identify the levels and explain. Name together every item of punctuation and review use of those known. (Teach unknown in Literacy Hour)	Peer support & by outcome (Individuals may have had brief input to prepare them, so are able to make a contribution, or may have LSA softly supporting)	OHT: 1:1	
3. Can we use what we have found?	**Short Activity: (15 mins)** Given Level 2 sentence on board – in 2s rewrite at higher level. (May need to be modelled first). This is more fun on A3 paper, (cheap – recycled?) or pupils' white boards, (PWBs). Show you / blu-tack round walls? As a class – discuss and identify interesting examples of 4 features. Select ideas and model composite/s on board. Name this 'UP-LEVELLING'.	Peer support & by outcome. Pair less able (LA) with higher ability (HA) OR pair LA together and provide adult support. Extension – add one or two sentences at a higher level.	newsprint / recycled paper OR PWBs pens Blu Tack if paper used	

Objective	Activity	Differentiation	Resources	Evaluation
	BREAK			
	Brief review of what has been said about 4 features of writing.			
1. Can we show what we know about punctuation and connectives?	**Activity: (25mins)** Hard copy of text excerpt = 1:2 Read text together first. Teacher first, then altogether for younger or less confident. Pupils – in 2s - identify elements of 4 generic targets using highlighters or by underlining. Give named colour for each of 4 and model on OHT or board first. Give answers. Share likes / dislikes about the passage and talk about suspense. Record interesting / ambitious words on board.	**Peer support & by outcome** Pair less able (LA) with higher ability (HA) OR pair LA together and provide adult support	Highlighter pens in 4 colours OR 4 colours of crayon / pen. Hand out & OHT: 1:2	
2. Can we identify features that show higher levels in writing?	**Writing Activity: (20+ mins)** Pupils write next paragraph/s to continue the story, copying the style of the writing. (Individual) Stop after ten minutes and ask who has used more than one type of punctuation, an interesting sentence opener, more than two different connectives, (if class understand the term) and an interesting / unusual word. Praise. Continue for further ten minutes, (or more if productive). Use back of hand out as needed.	**By outcome.** Pupils unable to write profitably without support should be given usual forms, e.g. scaffold, model words / phrases, adult support or work in a pair. (For last 2 it is useful to provide more privacy in a reading corner or shared area.)	Writing pens Hand out 1:2 Lined paper with margin	
3. Can we use what we have found?	**Plenary: (10 mins)** Collect work and explain will assess and return. Use the term 'assess'. Discuss meaning. Review learning on 4 features of writing – vocabulary, connectives, openers, punctuation. Review against today's objective. Use OHT of 'My Target Record' to explain how it works (1:3) – relate to 4 features. Say they will get it next lesson.	**Whole class.** Closed question/s for LA e.g. 'Is this a full stop?' 'Is 'and' a connective?'	OHT: 1:3	

> Six Lessons for Quick Impact
Lesson 2: Short Term Plan

EXEMPLAR MATERIALS – EDIT FOR USE

Subject: English Writing
Class: KS2
Date: Week 2

. KEY OBJECTIVE: to recognise and use the descriptive language

Objective	Activity	Differentiation	Resources	Evaluation
1. Can we show what we know from last lesson?	**Warm up: (15 mins)** What can they remember about the 4 features of writing? Collect actual examples on board, clustering into vocabulary, connectives, openers and punctuation. List 4 features, capitalise first letter to identify VCOP. Give pneumonic; Very Clever Old Person. Distribute 'My Target Record' and writing from last lesson. Pupils discuss how assessment and targets you set links to record. Publish key objective and discuss. Refresh use / content of Punctuation Pyramid. Activity: Give oral quick-fire sentences, pupils write the punctuation they would use, or use a punctuation fan to show and say.	**Group / adult support & by outcome** (Individuals may have had brief input to prepare them, so are able to make a contribution, or may have LSA softly supporting)	Handout 1:3 Last week's writing, assessed	
2. Can we identify descriptive words?	**Taught: (15 mins)** OHP: Lesson 2:1 Respond to text 'Howl…'. Identify VCOP features and collect on board. Link to assessment through 'My Target Record'. Brainstorm more descriptive words for monsters, (use language 'adjective' and 'adverb' when appropriate). Score goals. **Short Activity: (15 mins)** Distribute handout – Lesson 2:2 'Monsters' excerpts. Pupils read softly in 2s and choose ONE excerpt. Use highlighters or coloured pencils/pens to underline descriptive words (and record on scrap paper – optional). Collect on board. **BREAK** **Brief review of what has been said about 4 features of writing.**	**Peer support & by outcome** (Individuals may have had brief input to prepare them, so are able to make a contribution, or may have LSA softly supporting) Extension; do more than one paragraph OR extend chosen paragraph by one or more sentences Insert an easier paragraph to meet the special needs of your pupils.	OHT: 2:1 Highlighter pens in 4 colours OR 4 colours of crayon / pen. Hand out 2:2	

Descriptive
Eye Witness
(2004 ST)
It's My Fav. Meal
(2005 ST)

Six Lessons for Quick Impact
Lesson 2: Short Term Plan cont

Objective	Activity	Differentiation	Resources	Evaluation
3. Can we identify the VCOP?	**Short Activity: (15 mins)** Pupils practise, then read chosen piece to class in pairs, with expression. Discuss features of text that help to inform expression. Use highlighters / underlining to identify VCOP features and discuss. Play 'Find the Word' (5 mins) – working in pairs to find the word in the paragraphs that means same as the phrase teacher gives. Score goals.	**Peer support & by outcome.** Pair less able (LA) with higher ability (HA) OR pair LA together and provide adult support		
4. Can we respond to a descriptive text?	**Taught: (5mins)** Hard copy of text excerpt = Lesson 2:1 Pupils – in 2s - read together. Read together as a class. Share likes / dislikes about the passage and talk about suspense…. Tell them they are going to continue the story. Review collections of words / phrases on board from activities above.	**Peer support & by outcome** Pair less able (LA) with higher ability (HA) OR pair LA together and provide adult support	OHT & Handout 2:1	
6. Can we say what we have learnt?	**Writing Activity: (20+ mins)** Pupils write next paragraph/s to continue the story, copying the style of the writing. (Individual) Stop after ten minutes and ask who has used more than one type of punctuation, an interesting sentence opener, more than two different connectives, (if class understand the term) and an interesting / unusual word. Praise. Score goals. Continue for further ten minutes, (or more if productive). Use back of hand out as needed.	**By outcome.** Pupils unable to write profitably without support should be given usual forms, e.g. scaffold, model words / phrases, adult support or work in a pair. (For last 2 it is useful to provide more privacy in a reading corner or shared area.)	Handout 2:1	
	Plenary: (10 mins) Ask the 'Who has used…?' question again. Praise. Collect work and explain will assess and return. Use the term 'assess'. Discuss meaning. Review learning against the day's objective. Read a chosen example from the class, (identified while pupils are writing). Ask pupils to listen and remember a good example of VCO or P and / or a favourite phrase / sentence. Use as model on board.	**Whole class.** Closed question/s for LA e.g. Read a sentence; 'Was that a question?' 'Was the monster big?'		

EXEMPLAR MATERIALS – EDIT FOR USE

Subject: English Writing
Class: KS2
Date: Week 3

KEY OBJECTIVE: to find features of good writing / to use features of good writing

Objective	Activity	Differentiation	Resources	Evaluation
1. Can we show what we know about the VCOP?	**Warm up: (15 mins)** VCOP – quick-fire examples…. Who can start a sentence with…..? Who can change the connective in this sentence to a higher level…? Who can name the punctuation at the end of this…? (see Lesson Support Materials; LSMs). Score goals. Review Punctuation Pyramid. Share 'published' excerpt from a pupil's work last week, preferably on OHT. Don't say it's one of theirs, (see Lesson Support Notes). Read together. Identify VCOP features. Disclose whose it is, if pupil has not identified. Publish key objective and discuss. Activity: Give quick fire simple sentences. Ask pupils (2s) to record the new opener they would put in front, or use an openers fan to show and say.	**Group / adult support & by outcome** (Individuals may have had brief input to prepare them, so are able to make a contribution, or may have LSA softly supporting)	VCOP Cards (8:2) OHT: 3:1	
2. Can we identify the VCOP?	**Taught: (15 mins)** OHT: Letter from friend to expelled pupil (3:2) Read together. Discuss layout of letter. Read again. Identify good features, focus on VCOP including descriptive language.	**Peer support & by outcome.** Pair less able (LA) with higher ability (HA) OR pair LA together and provide adult support	OHT: 3:2	
3. Can we use what we know?	**Short Activity: (15 mins)** Given simple sentence on board – pupils work in 2s to 'up-level' it using VCOP features. Then work together to write a 'PS' for letter, on individual white boards, (PWBs) or scrap paper. Share good examples. Score goals. **BREAK** **Brief review of what has been said about 4 features of writing.**		newsprint / recycled paper OR PWBs pens	

Objective	Activity	Differentiation	Resources	Evaluation
4. Can we identify features that show higher levels in writing? **5. Can we use what we have found?**	**Activity: (25mins)** Hard copy of letter 3:2 Pupils – in 2s - identify elements of 4 generic targets using highlighters or by underlining. Give named colour for each of 4 (GTs) and model on OHT or board first. Give answers. Share likes / dislikes about the passage. Discuss in 2s what MIGHT have really happened. **Writing Activity: (20+ mins)** Pupils write reply from expelled pupil, copying the style of the writing. (Individual). Stop after ten minutes and ask who has used more than one type of punctuation, an interesting sentence opener, more than two different connectives, (if class understand the term) and an interesting / unusual word. Praise. Score goals. Suggest use 'My Target Record' as a prompt sheet to support writing. Continue for further ten minutes, (or more if productive).	**Peer support & by outcome** Pair less able (LA) with higher ability (HA) OR pair LA together and provide adult support **By outcome.** Pupils unable to write profitably without support should be given usual forms, e.g. scaffold, model words / phrases, adult support or work in a pair. (For last 2 it is useful to provide more privacy in a reading corner or shared area.) Train all adults on VCOP and Level 2 of Criterion Scale.	Highlighter pens in 4 colours OR 4 colours of crayon / pen. Hand out & OHT of excerpt 3:2 Hand out 3:2 Writing pens Lined paper Target Records	
6. Can we say what we have learnt?	**Plenary: (10 mins)** Pupils use 'My Target Record' to estimate level of writing – in pairs. Ask, 'Who has used…?' question. Collect work and explain will assess and return. Use the term 'assess'. Discuss meaning. Read two short excerpts from pupils' writing, (selected while they are writing) and ask pupils why they think you chose them. Discuss VCOP features. Review against day's objectives. **Homework:** Pupils find an ambitious word. Must know meaning and be able to spell well enough for all to read. Can ask staff, (WARN THEM!) Next day, scribe on scrap paper with felt pen and blu-tack round walls, (over displays). All read round room together. Does anyone know what the word means / how to use it? If a pupil has found a word no one knows, and s/he knows the meaning, score a goal. Teacher scribes interesting words and displays on word wall, (see 'Display') If any pupil/s then use the new words in future work, (any lesson/subject) they score a goal.			

> Six Lessons for Quick Impact
Lesson 4: Short Term Plan

EXEMPLAR MATERIALS – EDIT FOR USE

Subject: English Writing
Class: KS2
Date: Week 4

KEY OBJECTIVE: to recognise features of good writing / to use features of good writing

Objective	Activity	Differentiation	Resources	Evaluation
1. Can we show what we know about the VCOP?	**Warm up: (5 mins.)** As for Lesson 3 – use VCOP cards. (15 mins) OHT of phrases / sentences from pupils' writing of last week. (4:1) Why have I chosen these excerpts? Pupils identify which feature peers have used. Return essays and compare targets. Insert in Writing Portfolios. Record today's key objective and discuss.	**Group / adult support & by outcome** (Individuals may have had brief input to prepare them, so are able to make a contribution, or may have LSA softly supporting)	OHT: 4:1 Display Albums as Writing Portfolios 'My Target Records)	
2. Can we use features that show higher levels in writing?	**Short Activity: (10 mins)** Give letter from self to pupils, (4:2). They edit in pairs, 'being the teacher'. Extension = They 'up-level' by inserting features of VCOP.	**Peer support & by outcome.** Pair less able (LA) with higher ability (HA) OR pair LA together and provide adult support	Handout 4:2	
3. Do we know the structure of a story?	**Taught: (15 mins)** Distribute 'Story Structure' cards, (see LSMs). Ask pupils with blue 3 part cards to come out and stand where they think they would be in a story, (or to peg card on a washing line where they think it would go.) Ask greens to come out and cluster content cards in the part of the story where they think it might come. Ask some to say 'What sort of…?' e.g. 'What sorts of 'Who' / 'Where' would you get in the opening?' Ask mauve to come out and attach emotion cards to content cards. Ask them to explain what sort of feelings there would be in the part they chose. (See LSMs 8:1)	**By colour code:** Blue = LA Green = MA Mauve = HA	Story Structure cards (8:1) Washing line and pegs?	
4. Can we plan a story?	**Planning: (10 mins)** Give title for unsupported writing, (E.g. past SAT ' You're in Charge'). Make a single bubble map or list ideas that 'spring to mind'. Discuss as a class. Make a planning map. (See 'Planning Writing')		Scrap paper, coloured pens or pencils, or PWBs and felt tips	

Objective	Activity	Differentiation	Resources	Evaluation
	BREAK **Brief review of VCOP - 4 features of writing, and of planning maps.**			
5. Can we use the VCOP in unsupported writing?	**Writing Activity: (40 mins)** Remind of use of 'My Target Record' as a prompt sheet, and story structure cards. Pupils write. Stop after ten minutes and ask who has used more than one type of punctuation, an interesting sentence opener, more than two different connectives, (if class understand the term) and an interesting / unusual word. Praise. Score goals. Continue for further twenty / thirty minutes, (or more if productive). With second review after fifteen, and five minute / two minute warnings towards end.	By outcome. Pupils unable to write profitably without support should be given usual forms, e.g. scaffold, model words / phrases, adult support or work in a pair. (For last 2 it is useful to provide more privacy in a reading corner or shared area.)	Lined paper. Writing pens Target Records	
6. Can we recognise good features in our partner's work?	**Plenary: (10 mins)** Pupils exchange writing with their writing partner. Read and identify interesting example/s of VCOP to share with class, or to give to you to read to the class. Relate to today's objective. Have we achieved it? Link to next lesson. Score goals. Collect writing for assessment.	Whole class For this plenary it is more manageable to pair LA and provide adult support		

> **Six Lessons for Quick Impact**
Lesson 5: Short Term Plan

EXEMPLAR MATERIALS – EDIT FOR USE

Subject: English Writing
Class: KS2
Date: Week 5

KEY OBJECTIVE: to recognise features of good writing / to use features of good writing

Objective	Activity	Differentiation	Resources	Evaluation
1. Can we show what we know about the VCOP?	**Warm up: (5 mins.)** As for Lesson 3 – use VCOP cards. (10 mins) OHT of phrases / sentences from pupils' writing of last week. (Lesson 5:1) Why have I chosen these excerpts? Pupils identify which feature peers have used. Return essays and insert in Writing Portfolios. Compare personal targets with those on last week's work – same? Changed? (See Lesson Support Notes). Record and discuss the key objective. What does it mean?	**Group / adult support & by outcome** (Individuals may have had brief input to prepare them, so are able to make a contribution, or may have LSA softly supporting)	VCOP cards OHT: 5:1 Writing Portfolios 'My Target Records)	
2. Can we find features of good writing?	**Short Activity: (15 mins)** Give handout of selected poem at right pitch for class, e.g. 'Mist and Moonlight' and use OHT (5:2) Read as class. In pairs - identify good / interesting features. Discuss as a class. Discuss how writer creates atmosphere / use of descriptive language. Read again.	**Peer support & by outcome.** Pair less able (LA) with higher ability (HA) OR pair LA together and provide adult support	Handout / OHT: 5:2	
3. Do we know the structure of a story?	**Taught: (15 mins)** Review structure of a story – use Story Structure cards for quick refresher. Discuss 'scarey' things, focus on nightmare. Collect descriptive words for scarey things. Talk about how atmosphere is created in scarey movies….setting, weather, time of day / night etc. Make up a simple class story using the SSC cards.	**By colour code:** Blue = LA Green = MA Mauve = HA	Story Structure cards	
4. Can we plan a story?	**Planning: (10 mins)** Give title, '_____ Nightmare'. Respond with immediate ideas as a single bubble or a list or other. Discuss. Expand into a planning map for the story. (See 'Planning Writing')		Scrap paper Coloured pens / pencils	

Objective	Activity	Differentiation	Resources	Evaluation
	BREAK **Brief review of VCOP - 4 features of writing, and of planning maps.**			
5. Can we use the VCOP in unsupported writing?	**Writing Activity: (45 mins)** Give title for unsupported writing and discuss. Use own school or local feature – park etc. as setting. (E.g., 'Usher Street Nightmare'). Remind of use of 'My Target Record' as a prompt sheet, and story structure cards. Pupils write. Stop after fifteen and thirty minutes and pass to writing partner. Ask who has used more than one type of punctuation, an interesting sentence opener, more than two different connectives, (if class understand the term) and an interesting / unusual word. Praise. Writing partners might do a quick check for each other's use of VCOP features. Score goals. Return work. Continue for further twenty / thirty minutes, (or more if productive). With second review after fifteen, and five minute / two minute warnings towards end.	**By outcome.** Pupils unable to write profitably without support should be given usual forms, e.g. scaffold, model words / phrases, adult support or work in a pair. (For last 2 it is useful to provide more privacy in a reading corner or shared area.)	Lined paper. Writing pens	
6. Can we recognise good features in our partner's work?	**Plenary: (10 mins)** Pupils exchange writing with their writing partner. Read and identify interesting example/s of VCOP to share with class, (or pass to you). Review against today's objective. Have we achieved it? Link to next lesson. Score goals. Collect writing for assessment.	**Whole class.** For this plenary it is more manageable to pair LA and provide adult support		

> # Six Lessons for Quick Impact
> ## Lesson 6: Short Term Plan

EXEMPLAR MATERIALS – EDIT FOR USE

Subject: English Writing
Class: KS2
Date: Week 6

KEY OBJECTIVE: to recognise features of good writing / to use features of good writing

Objective	Activity	Differentiation	Resources	Evaluation
1. Can we show what we know about the VCOP?	**Warm up:** (5 mins.) Review VCOP – play Punctuation Pyramid game, (see Lesson Support Notes) 2 simple sentences on board for pupils to quickly 'up-level' in pairs on scrap paper / PWBs. (10 mins) OHT of phrases / sentences from pupils' writing of last week. (6:1) Why have I chosen these excerpts? Pupils identify which feature peers have used. Return essays and insert in Writing Portfolios. Compare personal targets with those on last week's work – same? Changed? Quick use of punctuation fans / PWB and openers fans / PWB if time. Review Punctuation Pyramid. Share today's key objective and discuss.	**Group / adult support & by outcome** (Individuals may have had brief input to prepare them, so are able to make a contribution, or may have LSA softly supporting)	OHT: 6:1 VCOP cards Punctuation Pyramid Writing Portfolios 'My Target Record'	
2. Do we know the structure of a story?	**Taught: (15 mins)** Review structure of a story. Give subject for writing, (e.g. past SAT = 'It wasn't meant to end like that!'). Make single bubble response or a list of ideas. Discuss ideas. Use SSCs to make up outline of class story at speed.		Scrap paper Highlighters Examples of text	
3. Can we recognise paragraphs?	Use OHT of a piece of text, or pages in books, to review paragraphing.		OHT 6:2	
4. Can we use a mind map to plan?	Pupils make a mind map or other plan, talking with partners as work. Clearly identify structure of the story, either through way map is constructed, or by use of highlighters in 3 colours for opening, body, and end.	Peer support & by outcome. Pair less able (LA) with higher ability (HA) OR pair LA together and provide adult support	Scrap paper Highlighters Lined paper. Writing pens	

Objective	Activity	Differentiation	Resources	Evaluation
	BREAK **Brief review of VCOP - 4 features of writing and planning maps.**			
5. Can we use the VCOP in unsupported writing?	Writing Activity: (45 mins) Give title for unsupported writing and discuss. Remind of use of 'My Target Record' as a prompt sheet, and story structure cards. Pupils write. Stop after ten minutes and pass to writing partner. Ask who has used more than one type of punctuation, an interesting sentence opener, more than two different connectives, (if class understand the term) and an interesting / unusual word. Praise. Score goals. Return work. Continue for further twenty / thirty minutes, (or more if productive). With second review after fifteen, (has anyone started a new paragraph? Use mind maps to check have used their good ideas. Has anyone used exciting vocabulary?) Five minute / two minute warnings towards end.	**By outcome.** Pupils unable to write profitably without support should be given usual forms, e.g. scaffold, model words / phrases, adult support or work in a pair. (For last 2 it is useful to provide more privacy in a reading corner or shared area.)		
6. Can we recognise good features in our partner's work?	Plenary: (10 mins) Pupils exchange writing with their writing partner. Read and identify interesting example/s of VCOP to share with class. Review against the day's key objective. Link to the future. Score goals. Collect for assessment.	**Whole class.** For this plenary it is more manageable to pair LA and provide adult support		

> Next
Teaching Notes

Teaching Notes for 'Six Lessons for Quick Impact'

NB THESE LESSONS ARE WRITTEN FOR UPPER KEY STAGE 2 BUT HAVE BEEN SUCCESSFULLY TAUGHT THROUGHOUT KEY STAGE 2, AND IN A YEAR 2 CLASS WITH ADAPTATIONS. THEY SHOULD BE MODIFIED FOR THE NEEDS OF YOUR PUPILS. FOR BEST RESULTS SEE 'BIG WRITING DAY'.

1. These lessons are NOT necessarily consecutive. They may be taught on a 2 weekly or 3 weekly schedule with supplementary lessons in between, to match the pace of development of the pupils. Commencing the series in the early Spring Term still provides sufficient time for impact.

2. These lesson plans are purely exemplar plans and should be adapted for the needs of the class.

3. The handouts provided as exemplars are only exemplars and teachers should select models that are appropriate for their pupils. (See Lesson Support Materials)

4. These lesson plans must be taught in conjunction with assessment against the Criterion Scale, and Teaching Assistants involved should be trained in the progression within the Criterion Scale, especially Level 2.

5. These lesson plans are designed to take TWO sessions of approximately 45 / 55 minutes each to deliver. They can either be timetabled before and after break on one day, before and after lunch on one day, or over two days.

6. All timings are approximate and will be affected by the pace of teaching and the response, prior learning and ability of the pupils.

7. These lessons are intended to be 'pacey' with a series of mini-lessons or shifts in focus to maintain pupils' interest and enthusiasm. They should not include large amounts of writing before the second session.

8. After lesson 1 pupils should be given a 'Writing Portfolio' to keep their handouts and work in. (See Lesson Support materials)

> # Teaching Notes for 'Six Lessons for Quick Impact'
> ## Lesson 1

Also see Short Term Plan and 'How To Use Lesson Support Materials'

Resources:	Punctuation Pyramid
	newsprint / recycled paper (A3?) or personal white boards (PWBs)
	Felt tips
	Blu Tack if using pens?
	Highlighter Pens in 4 colours or 4 colours of felt tips / large crayons
	Writing pens
	Lined writing paper (KS1 = A5, KS2/3 = A4, both with margins)
	OHTs / handouts: 1:1 'Harry Potter',
	1:2 'The Monster',
	1:3 'My Target record'

Key Words: punctuation
connectives
openers
vocabulary
ambitious

Warm Up: Teacher's white board (W/B) only.

Quick-fire recall of all the punctuation we can name. Repeat for all connectives we can name. (Use familiar terminology and examples to achieve recall, but introduce these terms as you record). You and/or pupils record the punctuation and connectives known to them on the W/B. You may need to prompt them and give clues to cover a range. It is not necessary to get more than four or five examples to have made the point.

Ensure they understand the terms and use of 'punctuation' and 'connectives'.

Short Activity: Give pupils connectives fans, (see Lesson Support Materials LSM: 11) OR PWBs.

Do several quick-fire pairs of sentences asking pupils to show and say the connectives they would use to join them. Keep it simple, e.g. 'I got up late. I missed the bus.' 'I got up earlier. I caught the bus.' Illustrate two or three options on the board.

KEEP IT LIVELY!

Taught: **OHT 1:1**

Use OHT of the 2 contrasting passages written at approximately L4/5 and L2/3. Play 'Spot the Differences' – what makes the one higher level than the other? Use to establish the idea of levels and assessment. Show the Criterion Scale and say you are going to be assessing their writing. Identify differences in punctuation, openers, connectives and vocabulary. Use to establish idea that these are the four features that can easily make a difference in the level of pupils' writing.

KEEP IT LIVELY!

Introduce the Punctuation Pyramid. What do they think it means? Explain relationship to levels. 'If you only use full stops you are punctuating at Level 1. Name all pieces of punctuation. Ask pupils how each is used to Level 4 and exemplify if time permits. If not, do as a 'filler' at some other point in the week.

Short Activity: Newsprint / recycled paper or personal white boards, (PWBs)
Blu-tack if using paper

Given 2 simple sentences on the W/B – in 2s rewrite at a higher level as one sentence. Display.

(Paper can be blu-tacked over existing displays and carefully removed later.) As a class – read and discuss. Identify interesting examples of the 4 features. Model your own higher level/s on the board and discuss. Name this 'UP-LEVELLING'.

BREAK

Activity: Highlighter pens – 4 colours, or crayons. Hand out and OHT of 1:2
'The Monster'.

In 2s – highlight or underline examples of four features in the text, 'The Monster', using colour codes to show each. Demonstrate a few first on board. Early finishers could make up additional sentence/s in same style. Model the answers on OHT. Discuss the passage, sharing likes and dislikes – emphasise the suspense – how does the writer achieve it? Talk about language and punctuation. Record some of the interesting words on the board. Can the children suggest more a) from text b) from memory?

Main Writing Activity: Handout 1:2, pens

Children continue the story. Emphasise they should try to maintain the suspense. Stop after 10 minutes and ask who has used a) interesting / ambitious words, b) more than 3 different types of punctuation c) different openers and connectives. Praise and reward. Read out one or two good examples you have identified while moving round. Work on for minimum of ten more minutes, longer if pupils are able to sustain. Praise constantly for hard work / working atmosphere, (even if not yet ideal!) Some pupils in all KS2 classes may be able to complete the story, working on the back of the paper. Some may only complete a good paragraph. Upper KS2 should complete unless disaffected, in the early stages of learning English, or have special educational needs.

Plenary: OHT 1:3 'My Target Record'

Collect the work and explain you will assess. Use and define the term 'assess'. Review the 4 features of writing from the beginning of the lesson at good pace. Use OHT 1:3 – explain how it works / relates to 4 features, and that class will receive next lesson. Review objective of today – 'To recognise and use the four features'. Ask children if they feel they can. Praise. Introduce the term 'Generic targets' briefly. Give next writing lesson's objective: to recognise and use descriptive language and briefly link to today's writing.

NB: BETWEEN LESSONS 1 AND 2, ALL PUPILS SHOULD BE GIVEN A 'WRITING PORTFOLIO', (see Lesson Support Materials) IN WHICH TO 'PUBLISH' THEIR TARGET RECORD, EXCERPTS AND WEEKLY WRITING.

> # Teaching Notes for 'Six Lessons for Quick Impact'
> ## Lesson 2

Resources:	Highlighter pens in 4 colours OR
	4 colours of felt tips OR large crayons
	Lined paper with margin
	Writing pens
	WRITING PORTFOLIOS
	OHTs / handouts; 2:1 'Howl....'
	2:2 'Monsters in Stories',
	1:3 'My Target Record'

Key Words:
excerpt
assess
target
adjective
adverb
names of all punctuation on the Punctuation Pyramid

Warm Up: Teacher's W/B, Handouts / OHT – 'My Target Record'.
Last week's writing

Review 4 features of writing – what do they remember? Record on board, clustering into the 4 sets. Ask if anyone knows proper names now – record as titles for each set, then list in VCOP order with capitals at front:

Vocabulary   Connectives   Openers   Punctuation

Explain that a quick way to refer to these 4 features is the VCOP, and give pneumonic to help remember; 'Very Clever Old person' – ME!

Distribute pupils' own Target Records and use, with OHT 1:3, to review link to the VCOP. Put name on top of Target Record. Return last week's writing and discuss the 3 targets you have set for each pupil. Explain how these link to Target Record and VCOP. Explain some targets may not show on the Target Record because they may be special to that child, e.g. handwriting.

KEEP IT LIVELY! Praise last week's work.

Activity: Oral quick-fire sentences. Pupils write punctuation they would use on PWBs or use a punctuation fan to show and say. Keep it simple, e.g. 'What is that?' 'BANG!' 'All of a sudden.....'

Taught: OHT – 2:1 'Howl....'

All read text together from OHT. Ask pupils to identify examples of VCOP from text – collect on board. Make links to Target Records. Brainstorm more examples of descriptive words for monsters and collect on the board. Use terms 'adjectives' and 'adverbs' to define as you write examples, when appropriate. Reread the text.

Strategies for Immediate Impact on Writing Standards

Six Lessons for Quick Impact
Lesson 2 cont

Short Activity: Handout 2:1 'Monsters', pens or crayons in 4 colours

Ask pupils to read all 4 texts in pairs, softly. (Reduce number for pupils with SEN, or insert a simpler passage, if necessary). Ask to choose ONE excerpt they like. Use pens / crayons to underline descriptive words / phrases, using a colour code. Discuss. Collect new vocabulary on the board.

BREAK

REVIEW WHAT WAS DONE BEFORE BREAK

Short Activity:
Pairs practise reading chosen piece, then perform for class. Discuss how features of text inform the performance, e.g. ellipses for suspense / anticipation. Use pens / crayons to identify all VCOP by colour code. Discuss and give answers.

Play 'Find the Word' – you give synonyms/ phrases for words in the text and pupils spot which word it is. **ORAL ONLY – KEEP IT LIVELY!**

Taught:
Give pupils individual copies of the text 'Howl…'. Read as a class. Share the likes and dislikes about the passage and discuss how the writer creates suspense and atmosphere. Tell children they are going to continue the story as they did last week. Review the words and phrases collected on the board. Ask to use as much of the VCOP as they can and use their Target Record for ideas.

Main Writing Activity: handout 2:1, pens, dictionaries available for self-identified use.

For this part of EACH lesson, pupils unable to write without support or discussion might move to a shared area or similar, with a Support Assistant to help them. This enables them to talk and receive ideas. The Support Assistant will better help them to make progress if s/he is trained in the VCOP and in at least Level 2 of the criterion scale. If no support is available, these pupils might still work as a small group in a discrete corner where they can talk softly, and you can provide focused support and encouragement.

Pupils write the next paragraph, and complete story if able, using the back of the paper. As last lesson – stop after ten and twenty minutes. Ask 'Who has used….?' Praise and reward pupils who have used examples of VCOP discussed. Ask how many different types of punctuation they have used, how many 'ambitious' words, (explain term). Have they used a Level 3 or 4 connective or opener from their Target Record or the board? Read some good models to the class, identified as you moved round supporting, and referring pupils to their targets from last piece of work, explaining as necessary.

Rewards might be washed grapes given one at a time as pupils write. Score goals.

Praise for good working atmosphere, and for increased period of concentration.

> ## Six Lessons for Quick Impact
> ## Lesson 2 cont

Plenary:

Ask the 'Who has used….' question again. Praise all for the way they have worked. Collect work and explain you will assess it and return it. Use the term 'assess' and review its meaning.

Read an example from the class, chosen by you when pupils were working. YOU read it to ensure expression and accurate interpretation, glossing over small errors. This enables models to be taken from creative children whose technical skills are not yet fully accurate. Ask all to listen and remember an example from the VCOP they liked, or a word / phrase they enjoyed. Collect on the board. Praise and reward.

Review objective of the lesson – to recognise and use descriptive language. Has this child done that? Have we all done that? Explain next writing lesson's objective will be to find and use all the features of good writing.

Tell all we are aiming for 45 minutes of writing next time – and how it will be rewarded. After the lesson: record new ambitious words, examples of good openers and connectives on A4, neatly, and display at front of room round teaching point. Assess all writing using the Criterion Scale, and record sub-level on spreadsheet. Set 3 short-term targets for each pupil.

MAKE A 'GOAL SCORER OF THE WEEK' CHART FOR NEXT LESSON. LIST NAMES OF PUPILS FROM WHOSE WORK YOU ARE 'PUBLISHING' EXCERPTS AT THE BEGINNING OF NEXT LESSON.

Repeat each week.

Resources: VCOP Cards
Newsprint / recycled paper or PWBs
Highlighter pens or 4 colours of crayons
Lined writing paper with margin
Writing pens
WRITING PORTFOLIOS
GOAL SCORERS OF THE WEEK CHART
OHTs / handouts: 3:1 OHT you make of a chosen excerpt from one of your
pupil's writing from last week. Edit serious mistakes but do not
change language etc. (See example 3:1)
3:2 Letter to expelled pupil

Key Words: 'up-level'
writing partners

Warm Up: VCOP Cards

Review meaning of VCOP.

Hold up cards in turn, asking, 'Who can open a sentence with this?' 'Who can use this in a
sentence?' etc. Expect pupils to shoot hands up – work at good pace and use constant praise and
rewards, (washed grapes for goals scored?) See LSMs 8:2

Use OHT of one pupil's work from last week (LSMs 3:1).

**DO NOT DISCLOSE IT IS FROM SOMEONE IN THE CLASS. TREAT IT AS THOUGH IT IS
ANOTHER EXCERPT OF TEXT YOU HAVE BROUGHT IN.**

All read together. Identify VCOP features. Identify what they like in the text. Praise. THEN reveal
author, if s/he has not already self-identified. Praise. Show 'Goal Scorers of the Week Chart' with
names recorded.

Write objective on the board and discuss so all clear what we mean by 'features good writing'.

Taught: OHT 3:2

Use OHT 3:2. Read together. Discuss lay-out / features of letters, (these should already be familiar
to class.) Read again and identify good features with focus on VCOP. Record interesting / ambitious
words on board. Link to Harry Potter excerpt in Lesson 1.

Give simple sentence on board at level 2. Ask pupils to work in pairs to 'up-level' it, (raise the
level) through insertion of VCOP features, using Target Record if wish. Use paper or W/Bs to
record. On signal hold up to you, you spot and read out / praise, OR ask pairs to read out together.
Record one or two good examples. Reward and score goals. **KEEP IT LIVELY!**

BREAK

REVIEW WHAT WAS SAID ABOUT 4 FEATURES OF GOOD WRITING

Activity: Highlighter pens or 4 colours of crayon, pupils' copies of letter 3:2

Pupils receive own copy of the letter 3:2. Read together. Use OHT to model the colours for colour code to identify VCOP, and do one or two together. Pupils use highlighters / crayons to identify 4 features of good writing, (VCOP) by colour code. Discuss answers. Share likes and dislikes about the letter. Discuss in two's, (as writing partners), what they think might have happened that day.

Main Writing Activity: Lined writing paper with margin, pens, handout 3:2

Tell pupils we are aiming for 45 minutes of uninterrupted writing today, and how they will be rewarded if achieved.

For this part of the lesson, pupils unable to write without support or discussion might move to a shared area or similar, with a Support Assistant to help them. This enables them to talk and receive ideas. The Support Assistant will better help them to make progress if s/he is trained in the VCOP and in at least Level 2 of the criterion scale. If no support is available, these pupils might still work as a small group in a discrete corner where they can talk softly, and you can provide focused support and encouragement.

Pupils write a letter in reply to the expelled pupil, using the style of the model letter. Stop after ten minutes and twenty minutes to praise for working hard. Ask who has used more than 3/4 different types of punctuation? What were they? Who has used an ambitious word – what was it? Who has opened a sentence in an unusual way? What was it? Who has used more than 3 different connectives? What were they? Etcetera. Praise and reward. Score goals. Each time –

Tell class how much time is left. Encourage use of the Target Record.
Try to encourage completion of the letter in the time, and full use of the time.

You move round, supporting, and referring children to personal targets from last piece of writing. Explain any not understood. Have an extension ready for early finishers and a scaffold for those who are struggling.

Plenary:
Pupils use Target Record to estimate level of own writing. (Work with writing partner if helpful). Protect self-esteem – no disclosures. Collect work. You read two good short excerpts identified as you moved round and supported. Discuss why they think you chose them and identify VCOP features. Praise all. Explain will assess and return to put in writing portfolios, then how pupils should examine personal targets on returned pieces and compare to previous writing. Model. Review learning against the day's objectives.

After the lesson: record new ambitious words, examples of good openers and connectives on A4, neatly, and display at front of room round teaching point. Assess all writing using the Criterion Scale, and record sub-level on spreadsheet. Set 3 short-term targets for each pupil.

Strategies for **Immediate Impact** on **Writing Standards**

Six Lessons for Quick Impact
Lesson 4

Resources: VCOP Cards
Leading Goal Scorers Poster
Writing Portfolios (LSM 9) / Target Records
Story Structure Cards (LSM 8:1) (and pegs / washing line - optional)
Scrap paper or PWBs
Coloured pencils or felt tips
Lined paper with margin
Writing pens
OHTs / handouts: 4:1 Single line excerpts from selected pupils' writing from last week.
Chosen because exemplify good use of features. You edit slightly to
improve technical skills if needed, but do not change text.
4:2 Letter from you to pupils, (see example 4:2). These can be
copied 3 times on an A4 sheet, and cut up, to reduce the number of
sheets needed.

Key words: single bubble maps
planning map
structure
opening, body, ending
character

Warm Up: VCOP Cards, OHT 4:1

Use VCOP cards as in Lesson 3 for quick-fire responses with praise and rewards / goals. OHT of single
line sentences / phrases from your pupils' writing from last week, (see example 4:1), edited but not
changed in language. Ask pupils why you have chosen these excerpts – encourage them to quote the
word/s and name the feature e.g. '_____ is an ambitious word' or name the punctuation and its use,
e.g. 'She's used ellipses for suspense.' Praise and publish the list of pupils on the 'Goal Scorers of the
Week' poster. Explain how it is to be used. Return essays from last week, for insertion in Writing
Portfolios.

Quick use of punctuation fans or opener fans to show and say what would put into given simple
sentences as before.

Compare personal targets as last week, who has the same? Who has changed?

Say objective is the same as last week; ask what they think the objective is. Record on the board.

What does it mean?

Short Activity: 4:2 Letter from you to pupils, (see example 4:2)

Give copy of letter, one between two. Pairs edit the letter, 'being the teacher'. Extension / early finishers – 'up-level' the letter to a level 3 / 4 by use of the VCOP / Target Record.

Go through answers and collect any extensions for feedback later. Read one or two good examples out / model on board.

Taught: Story Structure Cards, washing line and pegs, (optional).

The story structure cards should have been made on 3 colours of thin card. I buy a marbled card in green, mauve and blue. On each card I write one word in jumbo black felt tip, encasing the word with a border or a cloud. (See Lesson Support Materials)

Example: **3 blue cards** = Opening, Body, Ending.

18 mauve cards = 3 of each story features e.g. what, when, why, who, where, how

10 green cards = 2 of each emotions e.g. thoughts, hopes, fears, excitement, relief

Numbers can be increased to include all the class if desired.

Cards can be laminated for constant use.

Washing line to be strung across the front of the room if used.

Give out all the cards randomly – blue for pupils with SEN first time.

Ask blue to come out first and peg on line/ stand at the front in the order they would come in a story. If standing, ask them to 'Make the story longer' - spread across the whole of the front. Explain that to make a story longer we have to put more into it. That's what we are going to do now – to fill the gaps in our story.

Mauve come out and place their card on the line by the part of the story they would appear in, or stand beside the part. Ask children to explain 'What sort of 'Mrs. / Mr. Who' are you?' Move children to another part and ask, 'What sort of 'Mr. / Mrs. Who' is s/he now?' E.g. a 'who' in the opening might be the hero or main character/s, the 'who in the body might be a monster or a secondary character, and the 'who' in the last part may be the mother, the rescuer or the main character again. Repeat for 'Mr. / Mrs. Where', 'Mr. / Mrs. When' etcetera.

Give out the mauve cards and ask pupils to attach them, or stand beside one of the character cards. Ask what sort of hopes the character might be having at the beginning, in the middle or at the end. Move cards around and ask how they change.

Six Lessons for Quick Impact
Lesson 4 cont

Planning: scrap paper / coloured pencils or felt tips

Introduce past SAT title e.g. 'You're in Charge'. Ask pupils to make a single bubble map, or list ideas in response to that title. What does it make them think of? Collect suggestions on the board and discuss.

Ask pupils to make a planning map for their story, (see 'Planning Writing'.)

Tell them they are writing the story after the break, and that they will be able to do at least 45 minutes without a break. Make it sound exciting! Give lots of encouragement and praise.

NB Pupils should have had prior experience of single bubble and planning maps.

BREAK

REVIEW STORY STRUCTURE FROM PREVIOUS SESSION

Main Writing Activity: Lined paper, pens, grapes

Review planning maps / good ideas for story and remind pupils how long they have. Distribute 5 grapes each and tell pupils they may eat them whenever they like during the session as long as there are none left at the end. (This is purely to avoid 'misuse' outside the classroom!) While they write, move round giving support and discussing the personal targets on last week's work. At fifteen and thirty minutes ask who has used good features…. as in earlier lessons. Give lots of praise and rewards. Give countdown to finishing time; five minutes, two minutes, one minute.

Plenary:
Pair with a writing partner and exchange stories. Ask to read and make suggestions or spot missing punctuation. Return papers for a quick edit and collect in. Ask who has a partner whose writing was really exciting with lots of good VCOP features. Link to the achievement of today's objective. You read out a good example, compensating for errors. Review objective – who feels they achieved it? Praise and reward. Explain next lesson with focus again on finding and using good features. Review the VCOP if time.

After the lesson: record new ambitious words, examples of good openers and connectives on A4, neatly, and display at front of room round teaching point. Assess all writing using the Criterion Scale, and record sub-level on spreadsheet. Set 3 short-term targets for each pupil.

> ## Six Lessons for Quick Impact
> ## Lesson 5

Resources: VCOP Cards
Writing Portfolios / Target records
Story Structure Cards
Scrap paper
Coloured pens or pencils
Lined paper with margin
Writing pens
OHTs / handouts: 5:1 Single line phrases / sentences from some pupils' last work,
try to cover all the class over lessons 4,5,6.
5:2 Poem 'Mist and Moonlight' or similar.

Warm Up: VCOP Cards, OHT 5:1

Use VCOP for quick-fire warm up as in lessons 3 and 4.

Use OHT to ask pupils why you have chosen these excerpts, as for last week. Ask pupils to explain, relating to VCOP or Target record.   Return essays from last week for insertion in portfolios. Compare personal targets as last week, who has the same? Who has changed? Say objective is the same as last week, ask what they think the objective is. Record on the board.

What does it mean?

Quick use of punctuation fans or opener fans to show and say what would put into given simple sentences as before.

Short Activity: Handout 5:2

Use OHT of a poem e.g. 'Mist and Moonlight'. Read as a class. Give as a handout. Ask to work in pairs to discuss, identifying features of good writing. Discuss as a class – how does the writer create atmosphere? Which words/phrases give good description? Record some on the board.

Read again as a class. **KEEP IT LIVELY!**

Taught: Story Structure Cards (SSCs)

Use Story Structure Cards for quick review of structure, as done last week. Discuss 'scarey' things. Collect descriptive words/ phrases for atmosphere and scarey things. Redistribute SSCs, and say are going to build a story together. Call out the 'opening' card. Who wants to attach themselves? Why? Give the start of the story as their examples e.g. 'I want to be the 'who' – it is Adam and his friends.' 'I am the 'where'. They are going for a midnight picnic in the....' Etc.

Make up a simple story together.

Planning: scrap paper, coloured felt tips or pencils

Give the title for writing, '_____ Nightmare', (insert the name of your school, e.g. 'Usher Street Nightmare', or of a familiar feature in your locality e.g. the park or the museum. Ask pupils to do a single bubble response to the title. Discuss what aspects there are that might be 'scarey' in the dark. Pupils expand/adapt bubble into a planning map for a story.

BREAK

REVIEW PLANNING AND VCOP FEATURES

Main Writing Activity: lined paper, pens

Praise for writing for 45 minutes last lesson, and encourage to do the same today. Distribute 5 grapes each and tell pupils they may eat them whenever they like during the session as long as there are none left the end. While they write, move round giving support and softly discussing the personal targets on last week's work. At fifteen and thirty minutes ask who has used good features.... as in earlier lessons. Exchange with writing partners to check use of VCOP for each other. Give lots of praise and rewards. Give countdown to finishing time; five minutes, two minutes, one minute.

Plenary;
Pair with a writing partner and exchange stories. Ask to read and make suggestions or spot missing punctuation. Return papers for a quick edit and collect in. Ask who has a partner whose writing was really exciting with lots of good VCOP features. You read out, compensating for errors. Review objective – who feels they achieved it? Praise and reward. Explain next lesson with focus again on finding and using good features. Review the VCOP if time.

After the lesson: record new ambitious words, examples of good openers and connectives on A4, neatly, and display at front of room round teaching point. Assess all writing using the Criterion Scale, and record sub-level on spreadsheet. Set 3 short-term targets for each pupil.

> Six Lessons for Quick Impact
Lesson 6

Resources: VCOP Cards
Punctuation Pyramid
Writing Portfolios / Target Records
Story Structure Cards
Scrap paper
4 colours of highlighter / pencils
Lined paper with margin
Writing pens
OHTS; 6:1 single line excerpts from last weeks writing,
      6:2 page of text from a book that has paragraphs, several other books / pages that show paragraphs

Key Words: paragraph

Warm Up: VCOP cards, OHT 6:1

Use VCOP cards for quick, fun warm up. Then play 'Punctuation Game'. Pre-prepared Punctuation Pyramid has number of items covered with post-its – what are they? Who can close eyes and say all Level 3? 4? 5?

OHT 6:1 Why have I chosen these excerpts? Praise all and reward / score goals. Publish 'Goal Scorers of the Week'. Return last week's writing and read out one or two good example/s. Praise all. If any have used paragraphs, score goals. Insert in Writing Portfolios. Compare personal targets with last weeks. Has anyone's changed?

Quick activity using punctuation and openers fans or PWBs to show and say what they would insert in simple sentences, (as before).

What do they expect the objective is going to be? Write on the board.

KEEP IT LIVELY!

Taught: scrap paper, Story Structure Cards

Use Story Structure Cards for quick review of structure, as done last week. Discuss meaning of the word 'twist' – how the unexpected can happen. Give past SAT title; 'It Wasn't Meant to End Like That.' Ask to do a single bubble in response. Discuss ideas. Redistribute SSCs, and say are going to build a story together. Call out the 'opening' card. Who wants to attach themselves?

Why? Give the start of the story as their examples e.g. 'I want to be the 'who' – it is me and my best friend.' 'I am the 'where'. We are going babysitting for the next-door neighbour....' Etc.

Make up a simple story together. Pupils may not need to physically relocate at this stage.

Use OHT 6:2 and other selected pages in actual books to ask, 'How many paragraphs are there on this page?' 'On this one?' Discuss what paragraphs are and how they are used. Repeat until satisfied that all can identify confidently. Link to opening, body and end of SSCs.

Planning;   single bubbles from 'taught' section, scrap paper, coloured felt tips or pencils

Give the title for writing, 'It Wasn't Meant To end Like That'. Refresh ideas. Pupils expand / adapt bubble into a planning map for a story.

BREAK

REVIEW PLANNING AND VCOP FEATURES

Main Writing Activity: lined paper, pens

Praise for writing for 45 minutes last lesson, and encourage doing the same today. Distribute 5 grapes each and tell pupils they may eat them whenever they like during the session as long as there are none left the end. While they write, move round giving support and discussing the personal targets on last week's work. At fifteen and thirty minutes ask who has used good features…. as in earlier lessons. Exchange with partners for quick check on use of VCOP features. Give lots of praise and rewards. Give countdown to finishing time; five minutes, two minutes, one minute.

Plenary;
Pair with a writing partner and exchange stories. Ask to read and make suggestions or spot missing punctuation. Return papers for a quick edit and collect in. Ask who has a partner whose writing was really exciting with lots of good VCOP features. You read out, compensating for errors. Review objective – who feels they achieved it? Praise and reward. Explain next lesson with focus again on finding and using good features. Review the VCOP if time.

After the lesson: record new ambitious words, examples of good openers and connectives on A4, neatly, and display at front of room round main teaching point. Assess all writing using the Criterion Scale, and record sub-level on spreadsheet. Set 3 short-term targets for each pupil.

> **Next
Lesson Support
Materials**

Lesson Support
Materials

> ## Lesson Support Materials

These materials are designed for use within the lessons used to target raising standards in writing. They could also be used as quick warm-ups and 'fillers' at other times during the week. These materials are of three types:

Handouts and overhead transparencies, (OHTs), which should be reproduced on A4 using ICT. Handouts should be retained in pupils' Writing Portfolios and re-used or referred to in subsequent consolidation lessons.

Cards and posters, which should be reproduced on pastel coloured card using jumbo markers, and when possible should be laminated. They should become an integral, ongoing part of your teaching toolkit.

Resources such as the Writing Portfolio, for use in the lessons.

ALL LESSON PLANS AND MATERIALS ARE INTENDED TO BE ADAPTED AND ADJUSTED TO SUIT THE NEEDS OF YOUR PARTICULAR PUPILS.

1:1 Harry Potter Excerpt: OHT

Ask pupils to read it in 2s softly, then read as a whole class. Ask them to discuss – 'What is the same and what is different between the two excerpts?'

Pupils will usually recognise that it is the same part of a story written in a different way, and may use phrases that show recognition that the top text is easier or less interesting than the bottom one. They will usually correctly identify the source of the bottom text, and the author.

Lead the discussion towards text being written at different levels, like their own writing. Refresh knowledge of what the levels mean, with Level 4 being what we aim for in national tests at eleven.

Ask the pupils what level they think the bottom text is written at, then tell them it is Level 5. Ask what level they think the top is written at. Tell them it is mainly high level 2 / 3. Ask them which two words make it more definitely Level 3, then tell them if not guessed; '…. as if….'.

Pupils will usually suggest longer words here, e.g. 'recognised', as they assume higher-level words will be longer words. Use this as an opportunity to explain that 'ambitious words' are the only age related criteria. Explain that 'recognised' would only be ambitious if used by a young child of around six years old.

Discuss the words and phrases in the second text that make it a higher level.

Link to the VCOP.

Reinforce the point that the same basic piece of text can be written at a higher or lower level by use of the VCOP.

Use to introduce 'up-levelling' of simple text into higher-level text through use of the VCOP.

1. A man walked quickly down the castle steps. He walked as fast as possible towards the forest as if he did not want to be seen. Harry recognised him. It was Snape. Where was he going?

2. A hooded figure came swiftly down the front steps of the castle. Clearly not wanting to be seen, it walked as fast as possible towards the Forbidden Forest. Harry's victory faded from his mind as he watched. He recognised the figure's prowling walk. Snape, sneaking into the forest while everyone else was at dinner – what was going on?

Harry jumped back onto his Nimbus Two Thousand and took off. Gliding silently over the castle he saw Snape enter the forest at a run.

He followed.

The trees were so thick he couldn't see where Snape had gone. He flew in circles, lower and lower, brushing the top branches of trees until he heard voices. He glided towards them and landed noiselessly in a towering beech tree. He climbed carefully along one of the branches, holding tight to his broomstick, trying to see through the leaves…

Lesson Support Materials 1:1 'Harry Potter excerpt'

Lesson Support Materials
How to use Lesson Support Materials 1:2

1:2 'The Monster': OHT and handouts one between two
Read together from either OHT or hand out, whichever each pupil chooses. Use OHT pens to demonstrate underlining of VCOP features on the transparency.

Pupils work in pairs, using 4 colours of highlighter pens to highlight interesting examples of each of the four generic features, the VCOP.

Early finishers could make up an additional sentence in the same style.

Discuss features underlined, and express likes / dislikes about the passage. Discuss how the writer achieves suspense and anticipation. What do they feel might be going to happen?

Collect interesting vocabulary on the board. Can the class suggest more vocabulary that would fit in to this story?

Pupils write the next paragraph or continue and complete the story, according to their ability and attitudes at this stage. After ten minutes all should pause to discuss with a partner which features of VCOP they have used. The class should be asked, 'Who has used an interesting sentence opener?' 'Who has use an ambitious word?' 'Who has used a higher level connective?' 'Who has used more than 3 (4?) different pieces of punctuation?' Give a lot of praise and rewards such as washed grapes.

Praise for writing with concentration.

Consider having soft music playing during writing activities.

Consider providing water to drink for rehydration.

The Monster

With fear and dread I crept cautiously down the dark, damp tunnel. My hands were my eyes, nervously seeking the way by tracing the slime covered granite walls. Though I strained to hear and see, there was nothing....... nothing but the sounds of my own strained breathing and the soft pad of my rubber-soled shoes.

Suddenly an evil odour invaded my nostrils, like the rotting filth of a thousand corpses. I stopped, heart pounding. Was something there in the dreaded darkness? No longer able to stand not knowing, I pulled out my flashlight and switched on its harsh beam to light up the tunnel ahead.

Silence, heavy and still, surrounded me. Reassured, I began to step forward.... Out of the black depths came a sudden blood-curdling shriek as the great beast leapt towards me. There, pinned in the beam of my flashlight, I finally saw it....

_____

_____

_____

_____

_____

_____

_____

_____

_____

Continue on the back if you need more space.
Lesson Support Materials 1:2 'The Monster'

My Target Record
Lesson Support Materials 1:3 'My Target Record KS1'

Punctuation	Connectives
Level 1: I can use a few full stops, not always in the right place (.)	**Level 1:** I can join 2 sentences using any connective, e.g. **'and'**
Level 2: I can usually use full stops in the right place. (.)	**Level 2:** I can use 3 connectives: **'and' 'but' 'so'** I can sometimes use 'because' 'when'
I can always put a capital letter after a full stop (. A)	
I can try to use question marks and commas (? ,)	**Level 3:** I can use connectives to start sentences e.g.: **'before' 'after' 'if' 'as well as'**
Level 3: I can always use full stops followed by a capital letter, in the right places. (. A)	**Sentence Openers** **Level 1:** I can use simple words to open sentences: **'The...' 'My...' 'I...'**
I can always use question marks in the right places. (?)	**Level 2:** **I can open** sentences with words that show the order things happened: **'First...' 'Then....' 'Next....' 'Last..,'**
I can usually use commas and exclamation marks in the right places. (, !)	I can open sentences with simple connectives: **'But...' 'So...' 'Then...'**
I can try to use apostrophes in the right places to shorten 2 words **(isn't)**	**Level 3:** I can open sentences with harder words to show the order, (sequence) things happened: **'Also....' 'After...' 'Soon...' 'Another thing...' 'Because....'**
I can try to use speech marks. ("...")	

Lesson Support Materials
Lesson Support Materials 1:3

My Target Record
Lesson Support Materials 1:3 'My Target Record KS2'

Punctuation	Connectives
Level 1: I can use a few full stops, not always in the right place **(.)** **Level 2:** I can usually use full stops in the right place. **(.)** I can always put a capital letter after a full stop. **(. A)** I can try to use question marks and commas **(? ,)** **Level 3:** I can always use full stops followed by a capital letter, in the right places. I can always use question marks in the right places. **(?)** I can usually use commas and exclamation marks in the right places. **(, !)** I can try to use apostrophes in the right places to shorten 2 words **(isn't)** I can try to use speech marks. **("...")** **Level 4:** I can always use commas in the right places for both lists and pauses **(,)** I can always use speech marks in the right places. **("...")** I can usually use apostrophes in the right places to shorten and to show belonging. **(can't, John's)** I can try to use other sorts of punctuation, **e.g.** **ellipses = (.........)** **dash = (-)** **colon =** **(:)** **semi-colon = (;)**	**Level 1:** I can join 2 sentences using any connective, e.g. **'and'** **Level 2:** I can use 3 connectives: **'and' 'but' 'so'** I can sometimes use **'because' and 'when'** **Level 3:** I can use connectives to start sentences e.g.: **'before' 'after' 'if'** **'as well as'** **Level 4:** I can use harder ways to start and to join sentences e.g.: **'although' 'however' 'besides'** **'even though** **Sentence Openers** **Level 1:** I can use simple words to open sentences: **'The...' 'My...'** **'I...'** **Level 2:** I can open sentences with words that show the order things happened: **'First...' 'Then....' 'Next....' 'Last..,'** I can open sentences with simple connectives: **'But...' 'So...' 'Then...'** **Level 3:** I can open sentences with harder words to show the order, (sequence) things happened: **'Also....' 'After...' 'Soon...' 'Another thing...' 'Because....'** **Level 4:** I can use harder connectives to open sentences: **'Although....' 'Besides...' 'Even though....'** **'Before....'** I can use interesting ways of opening sentences: **'After a while..', 'Meanwhile..', 'Before very long..'**

Lesson Support Materials
How to use Lesson Support Materials 1:3 i and ii

1:3 'My Target Record' KS1 or KS2 Hand out for each pupil

Pupils keep in the front / back of their writing portfolio.

They highlight those 'Can do' statements that they have evidenced in unsupported writing. These may be identified by pencil tick at first, until you have had opportunity to confirm.

They star targets they are working towards.

Pupils use their Target Record as a prompt sheet in the early stages of the initiative, getting ideas for VCOP features from it to use in their writing.

They may use it to help them to estimate the level they are writing at, or to 'up-level' a piece of text.

> # Lesson Support Materials
How to use Lesson Support Materials 2:1

**2:1 'Howl...'   OHT and handout for each pupil
Use OHT only to open.**

1. All read text together from OHT. Ask pupils to identify examples of VCOP from the text – collect interesting examples on the board and later use in class collection / display, (see 'The writing environment').

Pupils use Target Records to make links, with support.

E.g.			
Vocabulary	=	'valiantly', 'teeming', 'throng', 'frantically' (10+)	
Connectives	=	'before', 'after', 'when' (L3)	'as' (L4)
Openers	=	'All', 'After' (L3) 'Valiantly', 'Strangely', (L5)	
Punctuation	=	? , 'x' !	.... (L4)

As adjectives, (e.g. ambitious vocabulary = 'demented'), and adverbs, (e.g. 'Valiantly', 'frantically') are collected, use the technical terminology. Add later to display.   Reread the text together.

**NB: Some words will fit into more than one VCOP feature and should be recorded in both if offered for both, e.g. 'Valiantly' = ambitious vocabulary and opener.
The two parts of this activity are divided by work on Handout 2:2**

2. Give each pupil a handout of 'Howl....' Discuss features pupils like / dislike.

Discuss ways the writer creates suspense and atmosphere. Review the examples collected earlier. Remind pupils to use the VCOP and their Target Records to help them to write.

Tell pupils how long they will have, and at what points you will pause for review.

Praise for how well they did last lesson, and tell them how well you know they are going to do this time. Pupils write the next paragraph and continue the story as appropriate for ability and attitude. Encourage those previously disaffected by writing, with frequent praise and short stops for quiet discussion and encouragement from you and another adult.

After ten minutes pause to discuss with a partner which features of VCOP they have used. Ask, 'Who has used an interesting sentence opener?' 'Who has used an ambitious word?' 'Who has used a higher level connective?' 'Who has used more than 3 (4?) different pieces of punctuation?' Give praise and rewards such as washed grapes. Praise for writing with concentration. Read out excerpts that show good use of VCOP.

Consider providing drinking water and music during writing activities.

Howl....

Who would have thought such small creatures could have made so much noise? Valiantly I struggled on, clearing a path through the teeming throng of tiny people as they rushed frantically away from the entrance to the temple.

'Turn back,' they cried. 'Turn back before it is too late!' But I had no choice. I had to press on into the gloomy stillness, the lives of too many were depending on the success of my mission.

Strangely, the inside seemed peaceful after the panic and confusion of the outside. I stood quietly, adjusting to the semi-darkness and listening carefully for any sound that would reveal the whereabouts of my foe. All was quiet.... too quiet! I waited.

After what seemed to be a very long time, but in reality might only have been a few minutes, I crept forward, picking a careful path between the tumble of chairs and prayer books scattered by the tiny people in their fearful flight. Not a sound did I make, as I approached the doors to the crypt at the back of the temple. My hand was resting on the giant iron handle when through the vaulted ceiling echoed the demented scream of a tortured spirit, rippling and bursting from the shadowed depths of the towering bell tower. It was the cry of the Mangee..... the haunted howl of death.

_____

_____

_____

_____

_____

_____

_____

_____

_____

_____

Continue on the back if you need more space
Lesson Support Materials 2:1 'Howl....'

Lesson Support Materials
How to use Lesson Support Materials 2:2

2:2 'Monsters in Stories' Handout for each pupil

1. Pupils read the texts softly, in pairs.

Each pair choose one excerpt that they like.

Use highlighter pens or pencil to identify descriptive words and phrases, e.g. 'wide tract of open country', 'gaunt pillar of black stone'.

Record new ambitious vocabulary on the board, e.g. 'tract', 'gaunt' and add to class collection / display.

NB in the lesson plan the two parts of this exercise are divided by break.

2. Review what was done before the break.

Each pair practises reading their chosen excerpt, softly. Stress use of punctuation and language to inform expressive reading. Pairs perform in rota round the room.

Discuss ways the features of text informed the reading. Link to ways they should use reading of their own writing to check for use of VCOP, and especially punctuation.

Working in 2s, pupils use 4 colours of highlighter or pencil crayons to identify VCOP features by colour code.

Discuss outcomes.

Play 'Find The Word'; you give synonyms and phrases for words in the text. Pupils find the word. E.g. You give 'swallowing hard' and they find 'gulping'.

MONSTERS IN STORIES

1. After days and days of journeying they came to a wide tract of open country, in the midst of which they found a gaunt pillar of black stone like a furnace chimney, and sunk to his armpits in the pillar there was a creature the like of which none had seen before. He had two great wings and four limbs, two like human arms and two like lion's paws, with claws of iron. The whole of his body was burned black from the desert sun, his hair hung about him like horse's tails and his eyes blazed like coals, slit upwards in his face, while a third eye in the middle of his forehead gave out sparks of fire.
(The Tale of the City Brass; The Arabian Nights)

2. The boy swallowed the pearl. A strange burning feeling began to spread through him, from the tips of his toes to the hairs on his head. He ran to the river and drank and drank, gulping down water as fast as he could. But still he burned with the terrible fire. Then his body began to change. He grew bigger. His eyes bulged and popped. His skin became covered in golden-green scales. Horns grew from his head and wings sprouted from his back.
(The Dragon Boy's Pearl – Chinese Folk Tale)

3. Now Kaliya was no ordinary serpent. He had five huge heads, with five sets of poisonous fangs, and coils so strong they could crush you to death. Soon the river was filled with Kaliya's lethal poison. Deadly fumes rose from the water which bubbled and boiled, black and sinister.
(Krishna Slays the Serpent King – Indian Folk Tale)

4. Now Medusa had eagle's wings, claws of bronze, and scales instead of skin. She had two sharp bronze tusks on her face, and writhing snakes, twisting and hissing, instead of hair. Anyone who looked at Medusa's face was turned to stone.
(Perseus and the Gorgon – Greek Myth)

5. The Minotaur was a hideous monster, with the body of a man and the head and shoulders of a bull. It was savage and bloodthirsty, and thrived on human flesh. From deep in the Labyrinth's centre came a terrible bellowing. The ground shuddered and shook as the mighty monster stamped its feet.
(Theseus and the Minotaur – Greek Myth)

Lesson Support Materials 2:2 'Monsters in Stories'

Lesson Support Materials
How to use Lesson Support Materials 3:1

3:1 'Scoring Goals in Writing' OHT

Use OHT made of an excerpt from one of your pupil's writing from the last lesson, presented as though it is the work of a recognised writer.

DO NOT DISCLOSE THAT IT IS THE WORK OF SOMEONE IN THE CLASS!

Select for positive reasons / do the minimum editing to make it coherent.

All class read out loud together.

Ask why they were able to read it so expressively at first sight. Discuss ways the VCOP inform reading, especially punctuation and descriptive language.

Identify the VCOP features as a class activity, using OHT markers to underline, circle etc.

Identify likes and dislikes in the text.

Reveal who the writer is, if s/he has not already self-identified.

Praise and make a 'Goal Scorer of the Week'. Add good examples to class collection / display later.

Lesson Support Materials 3:1 'Scoring Goals in Writing'

> ## Lesson Support Materials
> ## Support Materials 3:1 cont

SCORING GOALS IN WRITING

As Herman stared he glared at Gripe. He was talking to a cat. A BLACK CAT! After he carried on walking. Just then a very strange and peculiar thing happened …i…i…it was Gripe, he was flying! He was going towards Herman… and he stared at him.

"Well well if it isn't Herman" said Gripe. "What are you up to Gripe?"

Select one pupil's writing from the previous lesson. Only edit the minimum for sense. Use as a stimulus for all pupils, to exemplify effective use of the VCOP and to boost self-esteem.

The example above was used in the following way:

The class were asked to read it out loud together. They were asked how they had known where to put expression into their reading, and successfully identified that the punctuation guided them. They were asked if there were any interesting words in the text, any interesting sentence openers and connectives? Not until the discussion was finished was the author revealed as being a class member. In fact Umran self-identified for this piece, showing delightful humour by saying, "I…i…it looks like my work!"

Lesson Support Materials 3:1 'Pupil's Work From the Previous Lesson - Umran'

Strategies for **Immediate Impact** on **Writing Standards**

Lesson Support Materials
How to use Lesson Support Materials 3:2

3:2 'Letter to Expelled Pupil'   OHT and handout for each pupil

1. Use OHT only for first part

Read as a class. Discuss features / lay out of letters. Is this typical? Would pupils make changes?

Identify VCOP features and record interesting / ambitious vocabulary on the board.

Add to the class collection / display later. Make links with the excerpt from 'Harry Potter and the Philosopher's Stone' used in Lesson 1. Remind about the process described as 'up-levelling' using the Target Record and VCOP features.

Give two simple sentences on the board. Model 'up-levelling', using ideas and suggestions from pupils. Give two new simple sentences. Ask pupils to work in pairs to join and 'up-level' them. Use felt tips to record on pupil white boards or A3 / 4 scrap paper. Either pupils turn PWBs to you / you read selected examples, or blu-tack paper round walls, or pairs read out in turn on a rota.

Praise and reward, (washed grapes?).
'Publish' good models through display after the lesson.

NB in the lesson plan provided the two parts of this lesson are divided by break.

2. Use pupils' handouts. Read letter again together.

Model use of highlighters or coloured pens to identify VCOP features on the OHT.

Pupils work individually to identify VCOP, discussing as they work. Discuss answers. Share likes / dislikes, pupils discuss in pairs what might really have happened. Pupils write a letter from Herman in reply to Harriet.

Tell them how long they will have, and at what points you will pause for review.

Praise for how well they did last lesson, and tell them how well you know they are going to do this time. Encourage those previously disaffected by writing, with frequent praise and short stops for quiet discussion and encouragement from you and another adult. After ten minutes all should pause to discuss with a partner which features of VCOP they have used. The class should be asked, 'Who has used an interesting sentence opener?' 'Who has use an ambitious word?' 'Who has used a higher level connective?' 'Who has used more than 3 (4?) different pieces of punctuation?' Give a lot of praise and rewards such as washed grapes. Praise for writing with concentration. Read out excerpts showing good use of VCOP.

Consider providing drinking water and music during writing activities.

Lesson Support Materials 3:2 'Letter to Expelled Pupil'

**The Northern School of Magic,
14th February 2002**

Dear Herman,

What a disaster! I couldn't believe it when I heard you had been sent home! Have you really been expelled? Undoubtedly the evil Dumpstone is celebrating your departure…. the malodorous little vermin!

However hard I try, I cannot believe you pushed our great visitor, Dumbledore, off the top of the old tower. Sadly, however, so many people say they saw you do it. How can that be? Fortunately, the bushes below saved the professor from instant death, although he will be in hospital for some weeks. In his feverish ramblings he cries out, "Save me, save me from this bat-winged demon! Save me from his blood stained fangs, his raging snarls….. save me….."

Write soon Herman, I beg you. I need to know what really happened that night on the tower top. Who was the evil demon? How did Professor Dumbledore come to fall from such a great height?

Your loyal friend,
Harriet

Lesson Support materials 3:2 'Expelled' letter

Lesson Support Materials
How to use Lesson Support Materials 4:1

4:1 (and 5:1, 6:1) 'Goal scorers of the Week' OHT and display poster
The example given is from lessons taught at Usher Street Primary, Bradford. The model should be adapted, using excerpts from the writing your class produces each week.

Use OHT to celebrate examples of writing 'at the target level'.

The beauty of this is that in the majority of pupils' writing there is a phrase or sentence that has a feel of the 'voice' and style we are aiming for. Thus pupils have exposure to many good models from their own work, have high self-esteem because their excerpts are being 'published' in the same way text is usually presented in literacy and writing lessons, and have opportunity to examine what the strengths are in their own writing and what we are aiming for.

Over two to three lessons every member of the class should have an excerpt published in this way, and be celebrated as a goal scorer of the week. This may mean low-level editing on your part to protect the esteem of less able or dyslexic pupils. For example, correct the spelling of basic vocabulary that most pupils that age would expect to spell correctly, or insert basic sentence punctuation. The language of the excerpt should not be changed. If necessary, by the third week, ensure a child who has not yet produced one phrase of note is given the support to do so.

1. Display the OHT and **you** read all excerpts with good expression. Ask pupils why they think you have selected these excerpts. Aim for answers that suggest things like; 'They are good.' 'They sound good.' 'They are a high level' etcetera.

2. Now focus on each excerpt in turn. Read as a class and ask what they think it is about that excerpt that you liked. Aim for answers such as use of a VCOP feature, repetition for effect, alliteration, dramatic description etcetera. See below for examples from my illustration of 4:1

3. Praise and reward. Show the poster made for display and explain there will be a Goal Scorers of the Week poster up each week, with space for more names to be added for excellent efforts during the writing session. Ask pupils to think of these models when they are writing themselves.

Example of Answers from Year 6 in Usher Street, in response to 4:1:

Excerpt 1:   'Vocabulary – dimmed' 'Vocabulary – glanced' 'Connective and vocabulary – whilst' 'Phrase – "I took a glance at the beast" is different' 'Vocabulary – beast'

Excerpt 2:   'Vocabulary – gigantic and cyclop' 'Use of ellipses – "It was a…a…"'

Excerpt 3:   'Opener – Suddenly' 'Use of ellipses for anticipation – Suddenly…'

Lesson Support Materials 4:2 'Goal Scorers of the Week'

GOAL SCORERS OF THE WEEK

"The light dimmed. I took a glance at the beast whilst I still had time." **Jessica.**

"It was a gigantic, green monster. It was a…a…cyclop!" **Carly**

"Suddenly… I saw a bright light!" **Umran**

"Although I might have killed it, it still…." **Daniel**

"I was deafened all of a sudden, my heart pounding…." Zeshan

"My heart was pounding….pounding so fast I couldn't breath." **Jemma**

"Hopefully someone would hear but no-one came." **Benita**

"Meanwhile I was standing very still…." **Weiling**

"How was I going to escape? Would the beast eat me?" **Sana**

"The big, sharp teeth, the horrid roar, the green and black scales, they made me tremble." **Rachel**

"It opened its mouth and let out a stomach turning, monstrous and terrifying roar." **Ashley**

"I ran, and ran, and ran even more…" **Danny**

"It had transformed into a giant, drooling dragon." **Andrew**

"The monster, or whatever it was, was too horrible to describe." **Danielle**

"When suddenly….the beam of my torch lost its power." **Adam**

"It was like a slimy, slithery, fearsome man." **Stephanie**

Lesson Support materials 4:1 'Goal Scorers Quotations'

4:2 'Be The Teacher' Handout one between two.

Give each pair a copy of the letter and ask them to 'Be the teacher' by correcting and editing.

Early finishers and higher attainers could extend by adding two sentences at a higher level, or rewriting the letter at a higher level. Remind them of the excerpt used in Lesson 1 that was written at two levels, and the way we 'up-levelled' sentences in Lesson 3. Remind them they can use their Target Record and wall displays for support. By this stage there should be stimulating collections of VCOP features on the target wall. (See 'The Writing Environment').

Go through the edits as a class, recording on the board.

Collect letters, watching out for good models of 'up-levelling' to read out and praise.

Mark later.

N.B. By repeating the "letter" three or four times on an A4 sheet, and cutting them into single exemplars, seven or eight sheets can supply enough copies for the whole class.

Lesson Support Materials 4:2 'Be the teacher'

21.03.02

Deer Students of Year 6,

Thank you for the writing you did last week it was very good and I thougt you did well I have assessed it all and I have gave you all target to help you to get better.

Sadly my own wrting is not getting any better I am woried that I shall be sack if i dont do better soon

Your frendly teacher, **Ros. Wilson**

21.03.02

Deer Students of Year 6,

Thank you for the writing you did last week it was very good and I thougt you did well I have assessed it all and I have gave you all target to help you to get better.

Sadly my own wrting is not getting any better I am woried that I shall be sack if i dont do better soon

Your frendly teacher, **Ros. Wilson**

21.03.02

Deer Students of Year 6,

Thank you for the writing you did last week it was very good and I thougt you did well I have assessed it all and I have gave you all target to help you to get better.

Sadly my own wrting is not getting any better I am woried that I shall be sack if i dont do better soon

Your frendly teacher, **Ros. Wilson**

Lesson Support Materials 4:2 'Be the teacher'

5:2 'Mist and Moonlight'   OHT and handout one between two.

Use OHT and handout together, pupils select the one they prefer to read from.

All read together with good expression. Identify elements that promote good expression e.g. punctuation, italics.

Ask to work in twos to identify features of good writing. Discuss as a class.

Discuss how the writer creates atmosphere.

Discuss which words and phrases provide description. Record on the board and add to class collections / display at a later point.

KEEP IT LIVELY!

Lesson Support materials 5:2 'Mist and Moonlight'

MIST AND MOONLIGHT

Dark in the wood the shadows stir:
What do you see?
Mist and moonlight, star and cloud,
Hunchback shapes that creep and crowd
From tree to tree.

Dark in the wood a thin wind calls:
What do you hear?
Frond and fern and clutching grass
Snigger at you as you pass,
Whispering fear.

Dark in the wood a river flows:
What does it hide?
Otter, water rat, old tin can,
Bones of fish …. And bones of a man
Drift in its tide.

Dark in the wood the owlets shriek:
What do they cry?
Choose between the wood and the river;
Who comes here is lost forever,
And must die!

Raymond Wilson

Lesson Support Materials 5:2 'Mist and Moonlight'

6:2 'Demonstration Paragraphs' OHT and several Big Books open at appropriate pages

NB: No exemplar provided.

Use OHT to focus on what a paragraph is and how we discriminate them in text.

Ask how many paragraphs can be seen on the OHT. How did you know?

Discuss how paragraphs are used.

Show two or three pages from Big Books / enlarged text and ask how many paragraphs there are.

Acknowledge pupils who already use paragraphs successfully and consider using their writing as models.

This can be extended within the lesson or at another time by asking pupils through the writing in their writing portfolio and use the convention (double slash = //) to demarcate potential new paragraphs. Give feedback.

Lesson Support materials 6:1 'Demonstration Paragraphs'

Lesson Support Materials
How to Use Lesson Support Materials 7:1

NB: LSMs 7 are not used in the six lesson plans provided but are useful extension materials for later lessons. Pupils much enjoy being part of the developing story.

These letters also provide models for ways the termly letter writing TAT can be adapted to incorporate other text types.

7:1   'Explanation Letter'   OHT and one handout between two.

Remind pupils about the letter used in Lesson 4. If available, (in Writing Portfolios?) reread together and discuss ways the class interpreted the events referred to in the letter. Explain that you are now going to use a series of letters from, Harriet to her friend, Herman, who has been expelled. Ensure all pupils know what this term means.

Use OHT and handout together, and allow pupils to choose which they read from.

Read together as a class, with good expression. Identify the elements that promote good expression, e.g. punctuation and sentence length.

In twos, discuss features of good writing, e.g. VCOP features. Add good examples to class collections / display at a later time.

Focus on the explanatory text within the letter. Link to work done in Literacy lessons on explanatory text. Review features of explanatory text. Identify ways this text exemplifies the features. Discuss the content. Discuss how the writer, (Harriet) has incorporated it into her letter. How has she created the links?

Use as a stimulus to write:
1. Write a letter to a friend incorporating explanatory text. This is best linked to work pupils are undertaking in other lessons. For example, they could be explaining why rules are useful in P.E., why it is important to incorporate features of a fair test in a scientific investigation, or the importance of health and safety processes in food technology, design and technology, art, science or P.E.

2. Write a letter from Herman to Harriet incorporating an explanation for why he had to use supersonic flight, even though he was not yet qualified. This will require EITHER pupils making up their own scenario for Herman to need supersonic flight OR pupils reading LSM 7:2 before they write.

Lesson Support Materials 7:1 'Explanation Letter'

The Northern School of Magic,
5th June 2002

Dear Herman,

What wonderful news! Everyone is thrilled to hear that you will be back with us next term. Whilst you have been excluded from NSM, we have had opportunity to work on our individual projects for the inter-house contest. I volunteered to brief you on mine so that you can be involved in the competition after the holiday. I strongly advise you to scrutinise the following with care, in order that we may win the contest.

Explanation for How To Enter the Super-sonic Broomstick Flying Time Warp

Super-sonic flight enables broomstick users to fly at considerably higher speeds and altitudes than other fliers, giving significant advantage in a range of situations. There are three main parts to entering the Super-sonic time warp. These are as follows:

- advanced flier skills
- favourable weather conditions
- the super-sonic technique

1. Advanced Flier Skills: Because the broomstick pilot has attended the ASF training school, (Advanced Flier Skills), he/she is able to manoeuvre with greater speed and precision than most. Therefore far greater control of the broomstick is maintained while going through the techniques / motions needed to enter super-sonic flight.

2. Favourable Weather Conditions: Super-sonic flight requires a period of complete atmospheric calm, (no wind, rain or other adverse weather conditions) for the flier to pass through the Subsonic Window, (the moment of entry to super-sonic flight). Excellent weather conditions are essential for safe passage through the window. SERIOUS INCIDENTS have occurred, (mainly accidents), caused by fliers attempting to pass through the window when conditions have not been good enough.

3. The Super-sonic Flight Technique: Bare feet are essential to achieve the streamlined shape for successful passage through the window. Only highly skilful pilots of AFS status should normally fly barefooted. The broomstick is flown at an altitude of 1,000 feet, at a speed of 35 km per hour in a southerly direction. Precision, (accuracy) is essential, with neither speed nor direction wavering. When a secure flight path is established, the pilot leans forward on the broomstick, placing the arms straight forward along the shaft with fingers touching in a point in front of the leading end of the shaft. The legs are now raised onto the broom behind, with toes pointed to stern, (the back) Rapid left and upward arm flick and shoulder lift will now whip the broomstick to the required angle and 30 degree turn which takes the broomstick through the window into super-sonic flight.

I hope you will find the above explanation useful, however I do beg you not to try it yourself, Herman, until you have done the AFS training straight after the holiday.

Your loyal friend,
Harriet

Lesson Support Materials 7:1 'Explanation Letter'

Lesson Support Materials
How to Use Lesson Support Materials 7:2

NB: LSMs 7 are not used in the six lesson plans provided but are useful extension materials for later lessons. Pupils much enjoy being part of the developing story.

These letters also provide models for ways the termly letter writing TAT can be adapted to incorporate other text types.

7:2 'Report Letter' OHT and one handout between two.

Return work from previous lesson. Use strategies from the six model lessons to celebrate achievement. Add good examples of VCOP features to class collections / display.

Use OHT and handout together, and allow pupils to choose which they read from.

Read together as a class, with good expression. Identify the elements that promote good expression, e.g. punctuation and sentence length.

In twos, discuss features of good writing, e.g. VCOP features. Add good examples to class collections / display at a later time.

Focus on the report text within the letter. Link to work done in Literacy lessons on report text. Review features of report text. Identify ways this text exemplifies the features. Discuss the content. Discuss how the writer, (Harriet) has incorporated it into her letter. How has she created the links?

Use as a stimulus to write:

1. Write a letter to a friend who has gone on holiday, incorporating a report from the local newspaper on something imaginary they have done together, or on something their class / school has done.

2. Write a letter from Harriet to Herman incorporating a negative report from the newspaper on a disastrous attempt at supersonic flight by Herman, that causes chaos in the town.

Lesson Support Materials 7:2 'Report Letter'

The Northern School of Magic
18th June 2002

Dear Herman,

How COULD you? I can't believe you went against my advice and attempted a supersonic flight! A terrible tragedy could have occurred. I enclose, below, a transcript of the report on the incident as it was published in 'The Northern Times'.

Mystery Meteor Defeats Invaders

Evil invaders were defeated this morning in a dawn raid on Gringotts, the favourite bank of all witches and wizards.. Masked attackers swarmed into Diagon Alley and attempted to gain entrance to the vaults where many wizards and witches keep their fortunes.

The surprise attack began while most of the residents of the alley were still asleep. Security guards report that they had already begun the process of unlocking security codes and barriers ready for the day, when the invasion began. Later, an official spokesman said that this was usual as nobody expected a goblin attack after daybreak. It is assumed that the invaders were goblins, although so far no further information has been made available.

Mystery surrounds the event which led to the defeat of the rascals. A sudden crack like thunder, and a violent flash led to a rushing roar that swept through the deserted, narrow alley, and the tunnels and vaults below the bank. All attackers in its path were bowled to the ground, where they lay stunned until the arrival of the guards who arrested them.

This evening, representatives of the Ministry for Information reported that they were unable to explain the phenomenon that defeated the criminals, but that everyone was very pleased that it had happened.

Of course, you are quite a hero with everyone here because they have guessed what really happened and how brave you are. For myself, I shall never speak to you again.

Yours truly,
Harriet

NB: LSMs 7 are not used in the six lesson plans provided but are useful extension materials for later lessons. Pupils much enjoy being part of the developing story.

These letters also provide models for ways the termly letter writing TAT can be adapted to incorporate other text types.

7:3 'Persuasive Letter' OHT and one handout between two.

Return work from previous lesson. Use strategies from the six model lessons to celebrate achievement. Add good examples of VCOP features to class collections / display

Use OHT and handout together, and allow pupils to choose which they read from.

Read together as a class, with good expression. Identify the elements that promote good expression, e.g. punctuation and sentence length.

In twos, discuss features of good writing, e.g. VCOP features. Add good examples to class collections / display at a later time.

Link to work done in Literacy lessons on persuasive text. Review features of persuasive text. Identify ways this text exemplifies the features. Discuss the content.

Discuss how the writer, (Harriet) has incorporated features into her letter.

Use as a stimulus to write:

1. Write a letter to a friend persuading them to join you in something you want to do, or persuading them not to do something you don't want them to do. This may be linked to school lessons / activities or to something outside school.

2. Write a letter from Herman to Harriet persuading her to forgive him, and to spend some of the summer holiday with him practising for their Advanced Flier Skills status.

Lesson Support Materials 7:3 'Persuasive Letter'

The Northern School of Magic,
22nd June 2002

Dear Herman

This letter is to persuade you to rethink your decision not to apologise to The School Council. Sadly, it is not likely that you will be allowed to return to NSM unless you agree to take this easy step.

Riding a Nimbus Two Thousand at super-sonic speeds before qualifying as an ASF pilot, (Advanced Flyer Skills pilot) is a foolish thing to do. The pilot might easily fail to get through the sonic window and the sudden loss of speed would cause him to stall and fall to the ground. Furthermore, evidence shows that novice riders attempting to get into position before making the sonic attempt often lose concentration and hit obstacles in their way. This is especially dangerous in built up areas like Diagon Alley.

Although all pupils at NSM admire the brave action that protected the savings of so many, the school has rules that need to be obeyed if pupils are to develop into professional witches and wizards. If all pupils disobey the rules the school will be thrown into chaos. It is certain that the Professor tried to protect you by referring the matter to School Council. However, the your closest friends were unable to get to the meeting, as they were in detention for letting the hopping frogs loose. Thus your enemy's mates were able to swing the vote.

There is no doubt the Professor now has no choice, and must abide by the decision of the Council. It is essential, therefore, that pride is swallowed and apologies are made. It is a small action to make in order to come back to school. If it is not done, your foul foes will have won and there will be no more Herman Clay at NSM.

Yours coolly,
Harriet

Lesson Support Materials 7:3 ' Persuasive Letter'

Lesson Support Materials
How to Use Lesson Support Materials 8:1

1. Sequence Words:	opening	body	ending	(blue?)		

2. Content Words: who   what   where   when   why   how   (purple?)

3. Feelings Words: hope   fears   thoughts   feelings   sadness   joy

Use jumbo black felt marker on pastel coloured A4 cards and laminate.

Use as a physical activity by distributing the cards and asking pupils to form a line OR peg on a washing line in story sequence – sequence words first spread across the front of the room. Then content words clustered round the part they might appear in. Discuss what sort of 'who' you might get in the opening, in the body and in the ending, then what sort of 'what' might happen in each part etc. Finally, attach feelings to different parts. Ask who might have feelings in this part and what sort of feelings they might be.

This exercise should be lively and fun. It helps to embed the sequence for visual and kinesthetic learners, whilst your questioning accesses audial learners.

Lesson Support Materials 8:1 Story Structure Cards

opening

body

ending

Who?

What?

Where?

When?

Why?

How?

Lesson Support
Materials 8:1 Story
Structure Cards

NB: LSMs 8:1, 8:2, 8:3 and 8:4 are visual aids that are used in the six lesson plans provided and should be used regularly as warm-ups / fillers in later lessons.

These materials should be made on thin pastel coloured card and laminated, (if possible) to ensure they retain their good appearance when in regular use.

8:1   'Story Structure Cards' (A4)

Use as a physical activity by distributing the cards and asking pupils to form a line OR peg on a washing line in story sequence – sequence words first, spread across the front of the room. Then content words, clustered round the part they might appear in. Discuss what sort of 'who' you might get in the opening, (e.g. hero / heroine and family / friends), in the body, (e.g. monsters, enemies, trouble makers) and in the ending, (e.g. rescuers, family, officials). Then what sort of 'what' might happen in each part etc. Finally, attach feelings to different parts. Ask who might have feelings in this part and what sort of feelings they might be.

This exercise should be lively and fun. It helps to embed the sequence for visual and kinesthetic learners, whilst your questioning accesses audial learners.

After 'playing' the whole 'game' once or twice, it is usually sufficient to hold up the cards one by one, or pass them out to pupils who remain seated. When all are confident with structure, the cards can be put along the top of the teaching wall, (see 'The Positive Writing Environment'). They then form a prompt or scaffold for pupils' writing as they work. (Curtis – repeat this text again in the Lesson Support Materials 8:1)

Lesson Support Materials
How to Use Lesson Support Materials 8:2

8:2 'VCOP Cards' (A4)

Use by holding up and asking, "Who can make up a sentence with…." for a 'pacey' oral warm up.

This exercise should be lively and fun. Pupils should be constantly praised and rewarded with 'training goals' or washed grapes.

1. Openers: Level 3 and 4 connectives (Also see 'My Skill Kit')
                  Adverbs

2. Ambitious vocabulary – examples from recent texts read

3. Connectives; from the Level 3 and 4 lists (Also see 'My Skill Kit')

4. The Punctuation Pyramid, (8:3)

Use jumbo black felt marker on pastel coloured A4 cards and laminate.

Use by holding up and asking, "Who can make up a sentence with…." for a 'pacey' oral warm up. This exercise should be lively and fun. Pupils should be constantly praised and rewarded with 'training goals' or washed grapes.

8:3 'Leading Goal Scorers' poster (A1 / 2) – laminated card or white board

Use to record names of pupils who have written particularly well, who had a line published in 'Goal Scorers of the Week' celebration or who make a particularly good contribution in a lesson. Do not confuse with quick 'training goals' scored in warm-ups and discussion work, which receive instant rewards e.g. washed grapes.

(See 'The Writing Ethos'). As pupils score more than one goal in a week they move up the chart, which is cleaned off weekly to allow a 'fresh start' for all.

8:4 'Punctuation Pyramid' (A3) see page 32

Use to illustrate progression in punctuation. Ask pupils to guess what the pyramid represents. Steer towards 'levels'. Name all punctuation, (consider asking if anyone knows more e.g. parenthesis or brackets, hyphen or dash). These may be added.

Refer to it every time pupils write in any subject. Play games by covering items with post-its and asking what is covered. Work towards pupils knowing level 5 by heart.

This exercise should be lively and fun. Pupils should be constantly praised and rewarded with 'training goals' or washed grapes.

If.......

When.....

Although.....

If only.....

Swiftly.....

Anxiously.....

Joyfully.....

debatable

Lesson Support Materials
How to Use Lesson Support Materials 9

NB: LSM 9 is the pupil's individual 'Writing Portfolio'. This is a very important part of the high profile you wish to place on writing, and the promotion of the self-image of being a 'published' writer, and therefore a successful one, (see 'The Writing Ethos').

Purchase a 10 or 20-pocket display album for each pupil. These cost a few pence over £1 at stationary stores, and when bought in bulk a discount can usually be negotiated.

Twenty pockets will hold 40 pieces of work back-to-back.

Use a piece of coloured card to divide the first ten (?) pockets from the second, to form two sections. The card may be personalised in an appropriate way by pupils.

Section 1 is used to display the Target record and the handouts provided in lessons.

Pupils can include a glossary of ambitious vocabulary in this section if you wish, taken from the short activities and from the target display that you are constantly updating, (see 'The Writing Ethos').

Section 2 is used to display pupil's completed pieces of work, assessed and with targets recorded, (see 'Assessing Pupils' Work').

Pupils enjoy making a cover page, and a spine label with their name on and the title 'Writing Portfolio' using cursive script fonts on the PC.

NB: The investment of around forty pounds to provide these portfolios is not considered excessive if the raising of standards is a high priority, however if a school feels they cannot afford this they may adapt pupil sketch books or assemble their own portfolios.

MY SKILL KIT

NB LSM 10 is not referenced in the lesson plans but may prove a useful tool for pupils to use when writing. It provides further support and exemplification to go alongside the Target Record, and can be used as a form of scaffold by pupils in Key Stage 2.

EITHER reproduce on thin card and laminate. Have available with dictionaries and thesauruses. If laminated, some pupils will enjoy using highlighter pen to track the examples they have used already, in order to check the breadth of range they have used.

OR copy on paper and give each pupil his / her own copy to insert in the front or back of their writing portfolio.

My Skill Kit

OPENERS FROM CONNECTIVES

When	'When I went to the shops I bought a book.'
If	'If I had had more money I would have bought a video.'
Although	'Although I ran, missed the bus.'
Besides	'Besides missing the bus, I dropped my shopping.'
After	'After I got home, I ate my tea.'
Before	'Before I went to bed, I watched T.V.'
Even though	'Even though it was late, I didn't feel tired.'
If only	'If only I had run faster, I might have got home earlier.'
Despite	'Despite getting up early, I was still late for school.'

OPENERS FROM SEQUENCE WORDS

First	'First I hung up my coat.'
Then	'Then I walked to the classroom.'
Next	'Next I took out my books.'
After	'After I took out my books I found my pencil.'
Soon	'Soon the teacher started the lesson.'
After a while	'After a while I felt very sleepy.'
Before	'Before the lesson finished I fell asleep.'
Meanwhile	'Meanwhile the teacher continued teaching.'
When	'When I woke up I didn't know what to do.'
Later	'Later she had to show me how to do it.'
Shortly before	'Shortly before the end of the lesson, I caught up.'
Shortly after	'Shortly after that she collected in the books.'
Finally	'Finally the lesson ended.'
Eventually	'Eventually we went out to play.'

OTHER GOOD WAYS TO OPEN SENTENCES

Using 'ing' words:

e.g.   'Having eaten lunch, we played out.'
        'Walking home from school, I found a kitten.'
        'Reading my book, I forgot the time.'
        'Riding my bicycle, I got home quickly.'

Using 'ly' words:

e.g.   'Noisily, I ate my breakfast.'
        'Happily, I ran to school.'
        'Anxiously, I looked for my books.'
        'Excitedly, I talked to my friends.'